Communication with Tourists Made Easy

You're Welcome!

Tae Kudo

You're Welcome!—Communication with Tourists Made Easy

Tae Kudo

© 2016 Cengage Learning K.K.

ALL RIGHTS RESERVED. No part of this work covered by the copyright herein may be reproduced, transmitted, stored, or used in any form or by any means—graphic, electronic, or mechanical, including but not limited to photocopying, recording, scanning, digitizing, taping, Web distribution, information networks, or information storage and retrieval systems—without the prior written permission of the publisher.

Photo Credits:
front cover: (tl) © MIXA/Getty Images, (tr) © Yosuke Tanaka/Aflo/Getty Images, (br) © John Sones Singing Bowl Media/Getty Images, (bl) ©Michael H/Getty Images; p. 15: © usako123/iStock/Thinkstock; p. 16: © kazoka30/iStock/Thinkstock; p. 23: © Jose Fuste Raga/Corbis; p. 31: © Ryan McVay/Photodisc/Thinkstock; p. 32: © woyzzeck/iStock/Thinkstock; p. 40: © amanaimages/Corbis; p. 47: © Bloomberg/Getty Images; p. 55: © beyond/Corbis; p. 67: © SamSpicer/iStock/Thinkstock; p. 68: © Lonely Planet/Getty Images; p. 75: © Bloomberg/Getty Images; p. 76: (t to b) © t_cherdchay/iStock/Thinkstock, © Will Robb/Getty Images, © vanbeets/iStock Editorial/Thinkstock, © Flaz81/iStock Editorial/Thinkstock; p. 84: (t to b, l to r) © PhotomanRichard/iStock/Thinkstock, © kent10/iStock/Thinkstock, © hichako/iStock/Thinkstock, © B.S.P.I./Corbis, © Koichi Kamoshida/Getty Images, © Clive Streeter/Getty Images, © xPACIFICA/Corbis, © Bloomimage/Corbis, © Yagi Studio/Getty Images, © John S Lander/Getty Images, © mchebby/iStock/Thinkstock, © The Asahi Shimbun/Getty Images; p. 91: © Rex Features/Pacific Press Service; p. 99: © Jose Fuste Raga/Corbis; p. 100: © Bloomberg/Getty Images; p. 107: © Alamy/Pacific Press Service

For permission to use material from this textbook or product, e-mail to **eltjapan@cengage.com**

ISBN: 978-4-86312-279-6

Cengage Learning K.K.
No. 2 Funato Building 5th Floor
1-11-11 Kudankita, Chiyoda-ku
Tokyo 102-0073
Japan

Tel: 03-3511-4392
Fax: 03-3511-4391

はしがき

「こちらでお召し上がりでしょうか、お持ち帰りでしょうか」
このような表現を英語で何と言うか学生から尋ねられたことが、本書の制作のきっかけです。執筆を続けるうちに、多くの学生が英語での接客やスモールトークに関心を持っていることを知りました。訪日する外国人旅行者の増加に伴い、今後も国内にいながらにして英語で会話をする機会が増えていくことでしょう。

本書のねらいは、ファストフード店やレストラン、コンビニ、駅前といった身近な場で出会う外国人旅行者と、学生の皆さんがスムーズかつ丁寧にコミュニケーションをはかれるようになることです。各ユニットにはロールプレイやスピーキングなどのコミュニカティブ・アクティビティが数多く用意されています。シンプルな表現を繰り返し練習しますので、英語に苦手意識を持っていても楽しく取り組むことができるでしょう。

また、日本人にとっては当たり前でも、外国人にとっては驚きや疑問に感じることが多々あります。そのような事柄を紹介するパッセージやアクティビティも各ユニットに掲載されていますので、外国人の視点でニッポンを見ることで、新しく何かに気づく良い機会となるでしょう。

本書による学習が、街角で出会った外国人旅行者とのコミュニケーションの助けとなり、その体験が学生の皆さんへの自信につながれば、そして願わくば、その旅行者にニッポンの良さを感じてもらえれば、著者としてこれ以上の幸せはありません。

末筆になりましたが、原稿執筆に際して丁寧なアドバイスをくださり、終始、お力添えいただきましたセンゲージ ラーニングの吉田剛氏、細かい質問にいつも笑顔で答えていただいた関西学院大学のMatthew Barbee氏、原稿全体の確認や貴重なフィードバックをくださった京都外国語大学のPenny Totsui教授、そして、最終原稿を隅々までチェックし、さまざまなアイデアをご提案くださったparastyleの飯尾緑子氏に心より感謝を申し上げます。最後に、いつも温かく励ましサポートしてくれる家族にも感謝の念をここで表したいと思います。

工藤多恵

Contents

Page		Title
3		はしがき
6		本書の構成と効果的な使い方

Page	Unit	Title
9	Unit 1	For here, or to go?
17	Unit 2	How many are in your party?
25	Unit 3	I'll be right back.
33	Unit 4	Would you like me to heat this up?
41	Unit 5	Your total comes to 3,240 yen.
49	Unit 6	I'm truly sorry for the trouble.
61	Unit 7	Do you have a reservation?
69	Unit 8	Wi-Fi is available in this area.
77	Unit 9	I highly recommend Sakura Restaurant.
85	Unit 10	Turn right at the first intersection.
93	Unit 11	Take the subway to Hommachi.
101	Unit 12	First, put money in the machine.

57	Review 1 (Units 1–6)
109	Review 2 (Units 7–12)
113	Scripts for the Roleplays
125	Checklist

Scene	Special Activity
ファストフード店での注文対応	Rice Ball
レストランでの来客対応	*Ramen*
レストランでの接客サービス	Chopsticks
コンビニやスーパーでの接客サービス	*Oden*
買い物や飲食の会計	Sign
商品やサービスへの苦情対応	Apology
ホテルや旅館での宿泊客受付	Japanese Inn
商業施設でのサービス提供や近隣情報の案内	Souvenir
旅行者への観光案内	Culture
道案内	Map Symbol
交通機関の利用案内や観光施設の情報提供	Transportation
券売機や電化製品の使用方法の説明	Controller

本書の構成と効果的な使い方

本書は12ユニットで構成されています。各ユニットのテーマは、商業施設での接客対応や街中での道案内など、職場やボランティア時、あるいは日常生活で外国人と接する場面を想定したものです。各ユニットのDialogueとListeningセクションでは2種類の状況が設定されていますので、同じテーマでも異なる会話表現を学ぶことができます。各ユニットのアクティビティの概要は以下の通りです。

Warm-up

Trial
ユニットで学習する重要表現を知っているかどうかを事前に確認します。ユニット学習後にも、これらの表現が言えるようになったか確認しましょう。

Useful Words
ユニット内で使う重要単語や語句を確認します。音声を聞いて発音を確認し、意味もしっかり理解しておきましょう。

Dialogue

Dictation
重要表現を含む会話を聞き、空所に適切な言葉を入れます。その後、ペアで会話を練習すると良いでしょう。

Speaking
重要表現を含む短い会話を練習します。さまざまな相手と繰り返し練習する中で重要表現を暗記し、楽しみながら自信を持って発話できるようになることが期待されます。

Listening

Dialogueよりも長めの会話を聞き、内容が理解できるか確認しましょう。初めに質問を読み、要点に注意しながら音声を聞いてください。その後、質問に英語で答えましょう。

Useful Information

ユニットのテーマに関連する情報や表現をまとめています。Roleplayに必要な語句が紹介されている場合もありますので、音声を聞いて発音を確認し、意味もしっかり理解しておきましょう。

Roleplay

Listening AかBのどちらかをモデルとした実践的な会話練習です。初めに巻末のScripts for the Roleplaysから該当ユニットのスクリプトを切り離しましょう。表面がModel Conversation、裏面がRoleplay Scriptです。アクティビティの内容はユニットによって異なりますので、指示文をよく読むようにしてください。ロールプレイ時にはそれぞれの役割になりきって、できるだけ相手の目を見ながら会話を楽しみましょう。

Reading

日本の文化や習慣などに関するパッセージを掲載しています。文中の"you"は「(訪日している)皆さん」という意味ですので、外国人旅行者になった気持ちで一気に読んでみましょう。質問には英文(完全文)で答えてください。意味がわからない単語がある場合は、パッセージを読み終えた後に辞書で確認しましょう。

Special Activity

ユニットのテーマに関連する事柄について、クイズ感覚で楽しむアクティビティです。何気なく使っている言葉や見慣れた標識などを、英語でどのように説明すれば良いか考えてみましょう。

音声ファイルの無料ダウンロード ▶ https://cengage.jp/elt/ListeningSpeaking/

 のアイコンがある箇所の音声ファイルをダウンロードできます。

❶ 上記URLにアクセスまたはQRコードをスマートフォンなどのリーダーでスキャン（➡❹へ）
❷ 本書の表紙画像またはタイトル (You're Welcome!) をクリック
❸ 本書のページで 音声ファイル ボタンをクリック
❹ 希望の番号をクリックして音声ファイルをダウンロード

For here, or to go? — Unit 1

▶ このユニットではファストフード店での注文に関する表現を学びます。

Warm-up

Trial 以下の表現を英語で考えてみましょう。

1. 「ご注文はお決まりでしょうか」

2. 「こちらでお召し上がりでしょうか、お持ち帰りでしょうか」

Useful Words 1〜8の語句の意味をa〜hから選びましょう。また、音声を聞いて発音も確認しましょう。 02

1. come with (　)　2. include (　)　3. medium (　)　4. order (　)
5. ready (　)　6. regular (　)　7. repeat (　)　8. set (　)

a. …についてくる	b. 含む	c. セット	d. 繰り返す
e. 準備ができた	f. 中、ミディアム	g. 注文する	h. 普通の

1st Dialogue

Dictation ファストフード店の店員と客の会話を聞き、下線部に単語を記入しましょう。

Clerk: Are you ready to ¹._____?
Customer: Yes. I'll have a cheeseburger ²._____.
Clerk: OK. The ²._____ ³._____ a burger, French fries, and a drink. ⁴._____ drink would you like?
Customer: Uh, I'll have regular coffee.

Speaking ペアを組んで以下の会話を練習しましょう。Customerは黒字部分を枠内の語句と入れ替えて注文し、Clerkはその注文を表に記入しましょう。さまざまなペアで練習を繰り返しましょう。

Are you ready to order?

Yes. I'll have a **cheeseburger** set.

Ex. *cheeseburger*

cheeseburger
hamburger
fish burger
grilled chicken burger
veggie burger
teriyaki burger

2nd Dialogue

Dictation 1st Dialogueの続きを聞き、下線部に単語を記入しましょう。

Customer: Also, I'll ^{1.}_____ onion rings.
Clerk: What ^{2.}_____?
Customer: ^{3.}_____, please.
Clerk: For here, or to ^{4.}_____?
Customer: For here, please.

Speaking ペアを組んで以下の会話を練習しましょう。Customerは黒字部分をFor hereかTo goのどちらかで答え、Clerkはその回答を○で囲みましょう。さまざまなペアで練習を繰り返しましょう。

For here, or to go?

For here, please.

Ex. (For here) / To go
For here / To go
For here / To go
For here / To go
For here / To go
For here / To go
For here / To go
For here / To go

Listening

A ファストフード店の店員と客の会話を聞き、質問に英語で答えましょう。　🎧 05

1. What type of set did the customer order?
   _____

2. What type of dressing did the customer order?
   _____

3. What type of drink did the customer order?
   _____

B Aの会話の続きを聞きましょう。設問1は下線部に単語を記入して答えを完成させ、2、3は質問に英語で答えましょう。　🎧 06

1. What did the customer order?

   A _____ burger set with a _____ and _____ dressing, orange juice, and a _____ French fries.

2. Is the customer eating in the restaurant or taking it out?
   _____

3. What did the clerk give to the customer?
   _____

Useful Information　🎧 07

[ファストフードの定番メニュー]
- cheeseburger「チーズバーガー」　● fish burger「フィッシュバーガー」
- grilled* chicken burger「グリルチキンバーガー」　● *teriyaki* burger「てりやきバーガー」
- veggie burger「野菜バーガー」　● hot coffee「ホットコーヒー」　● iced* tea「アイスティー」

  *grilledは「焼かれた」、icedは「冷やされた」という意味であるため、受け身形の"ed"にします。

[ドレッシングの種類]
- Caesar「シーザー」　● French「フレンチ」　● Italian「イタリアン」　● Japanese「和風」
- sesame「ごま」　● Thousand Island「サウザンドアイランド」

Roleplay

Student A スクリプト ▶ p.114

Clerk あなたはファストフード店のClerkです。スクリプトの下線部2に以下の情報を入れてCustomerに伝え、1、3、4はCustomerから聞いた注文にチェックをつけましょう。Clerk役を3回行いましょう。

	1	2	3	4
1st Time	☐ cheeseburger ☐ grilled chicken burger ☐ hamburger	Japanese, Italian, and French	☐ Japanese ☐ Italian ☐ French	☐ apple juice ☐ cola ☐ iced coffee
2nd Time	☐ cheeseburger ☐ fish burger ☐ *teriyaki* burger	sesame, Italian, and Caesar	☐ sesame ☐ Italian ☐ Caesar	☐ iced coffee ☐ iced tea ☐ milk
3rd Time	☐ fish burger ☐ grilled chicken burger ☐ hamburger	French, Japanese, and Thousand Island	☐ French ☐ Japanese ☐ Thousand Island	☐ apple juice ☐ cola ☐ milk

Customer 今度はあなたがCustomerです。スクリプトの下線部1、4に以下の情報を入れてClerkに伝え、3は自分が選んだドレッシングにチェックをつけましょう。Customer役を3回行いましょう。

	1	3	4
1st Time	hamburger	☐ Japanese ☐ sesame ☐ French	hot coffee
2nd Time	*teriyaki* burger	☐ Thousand Island ☐ Italian ☐ Caesar	apple juice
3rd Time	veggie burger	☐ Japanese ☐ Caesar ☐ Italian	oolong tea

Roleplay

Student B スクリプト ▶ p.114

Customer あなたはファストフード店のCustomerです。スクリプトの下線部1、4に以下の情報を入れてClerkに伝え、3は自分が選んだドレッシングにチェックをつけましょう。Customer役を3回行いましょう。

	1	3	4
1st Time	cheeseburger	☐ Japanese ☐ Italian ☐ French	cola
2nd Time	fish burger	☐ sesame ☐ Italian ☐ Caesar	iced coffee
3rd Time	grilled chicken burger	☐ French ☐ Japanese ☐ Thousand Island	milk

Clerk 今度はあなたがClerkです。スクリプトの下線部2に以下の情報を入れてCustomerに伝え、1、3、4はCustomerから聞いた注文にチェックをつけましょう。Clerk役を3回行いましょう。

	1	2	3	4
1st Time	☐ fish burger ☐ hamburger ☐ *teriyaki* burger	Japanese, sesame, and French	☐ Japanese ☐ sesame ☐ French	☐ apple juice ☐ hot coffee ☐ oolong tea
2nd Time	☐ cheeseburger ☐ *teriyaki* burger ☐ veggie burger	Thousand Island, Italian, and Caesar	☐ Thousand Island ☐ Italian ☐ Caesar	☐ apple juice ☐ iced coffee ☐ iced tea
3rd Time	☐ cheeseburger ☐ hamburger ☐ veggie burger	Japanese, Caesar, and Italian	☐ Japanese ☐ Caesar ☐ Italian	☐ hot coffee ☐ oolong tea ☐ iced tea

Reading

▼ 以下のパッセージを読み、質問に英文で答えましょう。

Enjoy Local Foods without Traveling Around

Have you tried a *bento* yet? Some *bentos* are so beautiful that they look like art. There is a great way to enjoy a lot of local flavors without actually traveling around Japan. You can do so by getting an *ekiben*, which is a boxed lunch sold at train stations. Local flavors and specialties can be found in an *ekiben*, for example, eel from Nagoya and oysters from Hiroshima. Many kinds of popular *ekiben* are available at some special *ekiben* shops. While *bentos* are sold everywhere, some mothers make a homemade *kyaraben*, which means a character *bento*. *Kyaraben* were first created for small children to encourage them to eat many kinds of ingredients. There are recipe books for *kyaraben*. Maybe, you can try making one! Also, there are special *bento* boxes that keep your food warm for a few hours. While visiting Japan, you can enjoy finding your favorite *bento* and eating many local foods.

NOTES flavor「味」 eel「うなぎ」 oyster「カキ」 encourage「促す」 ingredient「食材」 recipe「レシピ」

1. How can a tourist enjoy local flavors?

2. What is an *ekiben*?

3. What local foods can be found in an *ekiben*?

4. Why were *kyaraben* created?

5. What is special about some *bento* boxes?

Special Activity — Rice Ball

A 日本の伝統的なファストフードの代表格はおにぎりです。1〜10の具材の説明をa〜jから選んで線で結びましょう。

1. いくら
2. 梅
3. エビマヨ
4. おかか
5. 黒ごま
6. 昆布
7. ツナマヨ
8. 明太子
9. 焼き鮭
10. ゆかり

a. sour pickled plum
b. dried bonito flakes with soy sauce
c. cooked salty salmon
d. tuna with mayo
e. salted and dried seaweed
f. spicy cod roe
g. salmon roe
h. shrimp with mayo
i. *shiso* leaf flakes
j. sesame seeds

B 選択肢の中から適語を選び、おにぎりの包装を開けてから食べるまでの手順を完成させましょう。

1. Pull #1 _____ down to the end.
2. Pull #2 away and off.
3. Pull the other _____ away and off.
4. Enjoy the rice ball _____ with _____ crisp dried seaweed.

corner   fresh   straight   wrapped

How many are in your party? Unit 2

▶ このユニットではレストランでの来客対応に関する表現を学びます。

Warm-up

Trial 以下の表現を英語で考えてみましょう。

1. 「何名様でしょうか」

2. 「まず始めにお飲み物はいかがでしょうか」

Useful Words 1〜8の語句の意味をa〜hから選びましょう。また、音声を聞いて発音も確認しましょう。

1. available (　)　　2. expect (　)　　3. follow (　)　　4. opening (　)
5. party (　)　　6. reservation (　)　　7. start with (　)　　8. wait for (　)

a. …を待つ	b. (予定の人物を) 待ち望む	c. ついて行く	d. まず…で始める
e. グループ、団体	f. 空席	g. 予約	h. 利用できる、空いている

1st Dialogue

Dictation 客とレストランのホールスタッフの会話を聞き、下線部に単語を記入しましょう。

Guest: Do you have any ¹._____?

Server: Sorry, all of our tables are ²._____ now. How many are in your party?

Guest: Three.

Server: Could you please ³._____ for about 20 minutes?

Guest: OK.

Server: Please write your name on this ⁴._____ _____.

Speaking ペアを組んで以下の会話を練習しましょう。Guestは黒字部分を自由に変えて伝え、Serverはその人数を表に記入しましょう。さまざまなペアで練習を繰り返しましょう。

Ex. *three*
_____
_____
_____
_____
_____
_____
_____

2nd Dialogue

Dictation 1st Dialogueの続きを聞き、下線部に単語を記入しましょう。

Server: ^{1.}_____ _____, please.
Guest: Thanks.
Server: Here is the ^{2.}_____. And, here is a ^{3.}_____ _____ for you.
Guest: Oh, thank you.
Server: Would you like some ^{4.}_____ to start with?
Guest: Could we have two glasses of cola?

Speaking ペアを組んで以下の会話を練習しましょう。Guestは黒字部分を枠内の語句と入れ替えて注文し、Serverはその注文を表に記入しましょう。さまざまなペアで練習を繰り返しましょう。

Would you like some drinks to start with?

Could we have two glasses of **cola**?

Ex. *cola*

cola
ginger ale
oolong tea
sparkling water
orange juice
lemon soda

Listening

A レストランのホールスタッフと客の会話を聞き、質問に英語で答えましょう。

1. How many are in his party?

2. Which seats did the party prefer, smoking, or non-smoking?

3. How long will the party wait for a table?

B レストランのホールスタッフと客の会話を聞き、質問に英語で答えましょう。

1. For how many and what time did the guests make a reservation?

2. What two things did the server offer Ms. Johnson?

3. What drink did the guests order to start with?

Useful Information

["water" だけが「水」ではない?!]

レストランで水を注文すると、特にヨーロッパでは "No gas or with gas?" と尋ねられることがあります。この場合の "gas" は「ガス、ガソリン」ではなく「炭酸」ですので、「水か炭酸水のどちら?」という意味になります。"Still or sparkling?" と質問されることもありますが、この "still" には「じっとした、静かな」という意味があり、ここでは「泡立たない」つまり「普通の水」を意味します。また、"Would you like a refill?" と聞かれたら、"refill" は「無料のお代わり」ですから、"Yes, please." と答えると良いでしょう

Roleplay

Student A スクリプト ▶ p.114

Server あなたはレストランのServerです。スクリプトの下線部2、4には以下の情報を入れてGuestに伝えましょう。1にはGuestから聞いた人数を記入し、Waiting Listには名前を書いてもらいましょう。Server役を3回行いましょう。

	1	2	4	Waiting List
1st Time		smoking	20	
2nd Time		non-smoking	15	
3rd Time		smoking	30	

Guest 今度はあなたがGuestです。スクリプトの下線部1、3には以下の情報を入れてServerに伝え、4にはServerから聞いた時間を記入しましょう。Guest役を3回行いましょう。

	1	3	4
1st Time	Eight	smoking	minutes
2nd Time	Six	non-smoking	minutes
3rd Time	Three	non-smoking	minutes

Roleplay

Student B スクリプト ▶ p.114

Guest あなたはレストランのGuestです。スクリプトの下線部1、3には以下の情報を入れてServerに伝え、4にはServerから聞いた時間を記入しましょう。Guest役を3回行いましょう。

	1	3	4
1st Time	Five	non-smoking	____ minutes
2nd Time	Three	smoking	____ minutes
3rd Time	Two	non-smoking	____ minutes

Server 今度はあなたがServerです。スクリプトの下線部2、4には以下の情報を入れてGuestに伝えましょう。1にはGuestから聞いた人数を記入し、Waiting Listには名前を書いてもらいましょう。Server役を3回行いましょう。

	1	2	4	Waiting List
1st Time	____	non-smoking	30	
2nd Time	____	smoking	20	
3rd Time	____	smoking	15	

Reading

▼ 以下のパッセージを読み、質問に英文で答えましょう。

Sushi Going Around—Worth Trying!

If you want to try sushi for a reasonable price, you should definitely go to a *kaitenzushi* restaurant. *Kaitenzushi* is sushi on a conveyor belt. Many types of sushi, usually two pieces of the same kind, are on a small plate and go around all the tables just like at a baggage claim. First, a server will take you to a table. At the table, some cups, hot water, and green tea powder are available. You can make tea by yourself while you watch many different sushi going around. Please take any sushi you like. But, once you take a plate, you should never return it to the belt. You should also never return empty plates to the belt. If you do not see sushi you like, you can order it. Not only sushi, but you can also enjoy *miso* soup, *tempura*, noodles, and dessert. When you finish eating, call the server to count how many plates you have eaten from. Then, you can pay the cashier near the entrance.

NOTES ▶ conveyor belt「ベルトコンベヤー」 baggage claim「空港の手荷物受取所」 green tea powder「粉末の緑茶」

1. What is *kaitenzushi* in English?

2. How many pieces of sushi are usually on one plate?

3. There are two things you should not do at a *kaitenzushi* restaurant. What are they?

4. What else can you eat besides sushi?

5. Who will count how many plates you have eaten from?

Special Activity   *Ramen*

ラーメンは外国人旅行者にも大人気です。ラーメンの説明に必要な語句を確認し、1～14に該当する英語をa～nから選びましょう。

■スープ [Soup]

種類 Kind	とんこつ 1 ( )	みそ *miso*	しょうゆ 2 ( )	塩 salt
濃度 Body	こってり 3 ( )	普通 regular		あっさり 4 ( )

■麺 [Noodles]

食感 Texture	バリカタ 5 ( )	硬め 6 ( )	普通 regular	柔らかめ 7 ( )
量 Volume	大盛 8 ( )	普通 regular		少なめ 9 ( )

■トッピング [Topping]

メンマ
fermented bamboo shoots

もやし
10 ( )

青ねぎ
11 ( )

煮玉子
simmered egg

のり
12 ( )

コーン
corn

チャーシュー
13 ( )

ほうれん草
14 ( )

a. bean sprouts	**b.** dried seaweed	**c.** extra	**d.** extra hard
e. green onions	**f.** hard	**g.** less	**h.** light
i. pork bone	**j.** roasted pork	**k.** soft	**l.** soy sauce
m. spinach	**n.** thick		

I'll be right back.

Unit 3

▶ このユニットではレストランでの接客サービスに関する表現を学びます。

Warm-up

Trial 以下の表現を英語で考えてみましょう。

1. 「こちらは魚貝類と野菜用のつゆでございます」

2. 「すぐにお持ちいたします」

Useful Words 1〜8の語句の意味をa〜hから選びましょう。また、音声を聞いて発音も確認しましょう。

1. careful (　)　　2. dip (　)　　3. enjoy (　)　　4. meal (　)
5. mix (　)　　6. pepper (　)　　7. refill (　)　　8. soy sauce (　)

a. お代わり　b. こしょう　c. しょうゆ　d. つける
e. 楽しむ　f. 気をつける　g. 混ぜる　h. 食事

1st Dialogue

Dictation レストランのホールスタッフと客の会話を聞き、下線部に単語を記入しましょう。

Server: This is the Tempura Special. ¹_____ _____. It's very hot.
Guest: What is this for?
Server: It's the ²_____ for seafood and vegetables.
Guest: Oh, OK.
Server: Please ³_____ them in this ²_____. Enjoy your ⁴_____.
Guest: Thanks.

Speaking ペアを組んで以下の会話を練習しましょう。Serverは黒字部分を枠内の語句と入れ替えて説明し、Guestはその内容を表に記入しましょう。さまざまなペアで練習を繰り返しましょう。

What is this for?

It's the **sauce** for **seafood and vegetables**.

Ex.	*sauce*	for	*seafood and vegetables*
		for	
		for	
		for	
		for	
		for	
		for	
		for	

sauce / seafood and vegetables
sauce / buckwheat noodles
raw egg / beef and vegetables
powder / green tea
spicy oil / *gyoza*
soy sauce / sushi

2nd Dialogue

Dictation 1st Dialogueの続きを聞き、下線部に単語を記入しましょう。

Server: How is ¹._____?
Guest: Very good.
Server: Do you ²._____ anything?
Guest: Actually, ³._____ I have some salt?
Server: Sure. I'll be right ⁴._____.

Speaking ペアを組んで以下の会話を練習しましょう。Guestは黒字部分を枠内の語句と入れ替えて伝え、Serverはその内容を表に記入しましょう。さまざまなペアで練習を繰り返しましょう。

Could I have some **salt**?

Sure. I'll be right back.

Ex. salt

salt
soy sauce
sugar
pepper
napkins
ketchup

Listening

A レストランのホールスタッフと客の会話を聞きましょう。設問1、2は質問に英語で答え、3は下線部に単語を記入して答えを完成させましょう。 🎧 18

1. What did the server bring?
   _____

2. What should the guest dip in the sauce?
   _____

3. What will the guest probably try to do?

   He will _____ wasabi, _____ onions, and dried seaweed into the _____.

B Ⓐの会話の続きを聞き、質問に英語で答えましょう。 🎧 19

1. What did the server offer?
   _____

2. What did the guest ask for?
   _____

3. What will the server bring to the guest next?
   _____

Useful Information 🎧 20

[和食に欠かせない調味料や薬味]
- dried bonito flakes「かつお節」　● dried sardines「煮干し」　● dried seaweed「のり」
- garlic「にんにく」　● ginger「しょうが」　● green onions「青ねぎ」　● kelp「昆布」
- Japanese ginger「みょうが」　● mustard「からし」　● quail egg「うずらの卵」
- raw egg「生卵」　● sake「酒」　● seven-spice chili pepper「七味唐辛子」
- *shiso* leaf「しそ」　● soybean paste / *miso*「みそ」　● soy sauce「しょうゆ」
- sweet cooking rice wine「みりん」　● vinegar「酢」　● wasabi「わさび」

Roleplay

Student A スクリプト ▶ p.116

Server あなたはレストランのServerです。スクリプトの下線部1〜3に以下の情報を入れてGuestに伝えましょう。Server役を2回行いましょう。

	1	2	3
1st Time	Shabu-shabu	beef and vegetables	green onions and Japanese radish
2nd Time	Kamaage-udon	thick wheat noodles	Japanese radish, green onions, and ginger

Guest 今度はあなたがGuestです。スクリプトを参考にしながらServerの説明を聞き、自分が注文した料理について以下の1〜3の空欄に適語を記入しましょう。Guest役を2回行いましょう。

	1	2	3
1st Time	_____ Special	_____ and _____	Japanese _____ and green _____
2nd Time	_____ Special	_____ and Japanese _____	Japanese _____, green _____, and seven-spice _____

29

Roleplay

Student B スクリプト ▶ p.116

Guest あなたはレストランのGuestです。スクリプトを参考にしながらServerの説明を聞き、自分が注文した料理について以下の1〜3の空欄に適語を記入しましょう。Guest役を2回行いましょう。

	1	2	3
1st Time	Special	and	green and Japanese
2nd Time	Special	thick	Japanese , green , and

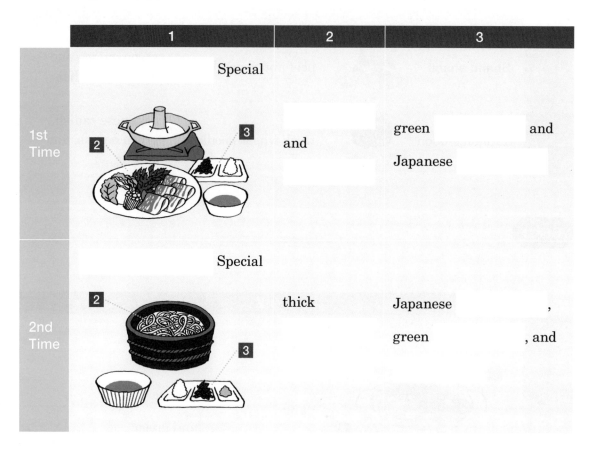

Server 今度はあなたがServerです。スクリプトの下線部1〜3に以下の情報を入れてGuestに伝えましょう。Server役を2回行いましょう。

	1	2	3
1st Time	Mizutaki	chicken and vegetables	Japanese radish and green onions
2nd Time	Yudofu	tofu and Japanese leeks	Japanese radish, green onions, and seven-spice chili pepper

Reading

▼ 以下のパッセージを読み、質問に英文で答えましょう。

When Can You Finally Enjoy Your Drink?

You may go to an *izakaya* where you can enjoy drinking and having a variety of food at a reasonable price. There, you may happen to see a group of Japanese business people in suits stand up straight holding glasses of beer with both hands. They all look at one person, probably their boss, giving a speech. In Japan, you are not supposed to start drinking until everyone has a drink, and someone, maybe the boss, makes a toast. After everyone says "*kampai*," which means "cheers," you should clink glasses with other people around you, and finally you can drink! You may be surprised at how patient they can be. Japanese people usually pour drinks for others. If you see someone's glass is empty, you can pour another drink for them. When you are offered a refill, you should hold your glass with both hands to show respect.

NOTES
happen to「たまたま…する」 *be* not supposed to「…すべきでない」 make a toast「乾杯する」
clink「カチンとならす」 patient「我慢強い」 pour「注ぐ」

1. What do people enjoy at an *izakaya*?

2. What is the group of Japanese business people looking at?

3. When are Japanese people allowed to drink?

4. How do you say "*kampai*" in English?

5. What should you do when someone refills your glass?

Special Activity: Chopsticks

箸使いにはさまざまなタブーがあります。選択肢の中から適語を選び、注意事項に関する英文を完成させましょう。

1 握り箸
Do not _____ chopsticks with all five fingers.

5 叩き箸
Do not _____ plates with your chopsticks.

2 噛み箸
Do not _____ your chopsticks.

6 指し箸
Do not use chopsticks to _____ to someone or something.

3 箸渡し
Do not _____ food with your chopsticks to someone else's chopsticks.

7 突き箸
Do not _____ food with your chopsticks.

4 寄せ箸
Do not use chopsticks to _____ plates.

8 ねぶり箸
Do not _____ your chopsticks.

| bang | bite | hold | lick | move | pass | point | stab |

Would you like me to heat this up? Unit 4

▶ このユニットではコンビニやスーパーでの接客サービスに関する表現を学びます。

Warm-up

Trial　以下の表現を英語で考えてみましょう。

1. 「お箸はいくつご入用ですか」

2. 「こちらを温めましょうか」

Useful Words　1〜8の語句の意味をa〜hから選びましょう。また、音声を聞いて発音も確認しましょう。　22

1. boxed lunch (　)　　2. chopsticks (　)　　3. fill out (　)
4. free (　)　　　　　　5. heat up (　)　　　　6. over there (　)
7. registration form (　)　8. separate (　)

　　a. …に記入する　b. 温める　　c. あちらで　　d. 登録用紙
　　e. 箸　　　　　　f. 分ける　　g. 弁当　　　　h. 無料の

1st Dialogue

Dictation コンビニの店員と客の会話を聞き、下線部に単語を記入しましょう。

Clerk: Do you need a 1._____?

Customer: Yes, please.

Clerk: OK. 2._____ _____ _____ do you need?

Customer: Two pairs, please.

Speaking ペアを組んで以下の会話を練習しましょう。Clerkは黒字部分を枠内の語句と入れ替えて質問し、Customerは希望の個数を伝えてからアイテム名を表に記入しましょう。さまざまなペアで練習を繰り返しましょう。

How many spoons do you need?

Two, please.

Ex. *spoons*

- spoons
- forks
- wet napkins
- packets of ketchup
- packets of mustard
- packets of soy sauce
- extra bags

Would you like me to heat this up?

2nd Dialogue

Dictation 1st Dialogueの続きを聞き、下線部に単語を記入しましょう。

Clerk: Would you like me to ¹._____ _____ _____?
Customer: No, thank you. Could I have two pieces of ²._____ chicken?
Clerk: OK. Anything ³._____?
Customer: Yeah. One small cup for ⁴._____ coffee, please.

Speaking ペアを組んで以下の会話を練習しましょう。Customerは黒字部分をYes, please. かNo, thank you.のどちらかで答え、Clerkはその回答を○で囲みましょう。さまざまなペアで練習を繰り返しましょう。

Clerk

Would you like me to heat this up?

Customer

No, thank you.

Ex. Yes, please. / (No, thank you.)
Yes, please. / No, thank you.
Yes, please. / No, thank you.
Yes, please. / No, thank you.
Yes, please. / No, thank you.
Yes, please. / No, thank you.
Yes, please. / No, thank you.
Yes, please. / No, thank you.

Listening

A コンビニの店員と客の会話を聞き、質問に英語で答えましょう。

1. What can the customer make for free?

2. What did the customer fill out?

3. What is available at the counter?

B コンビニの店員と客の会話を聞き、質問に英語で答えましょう。

1. How many donuts did the customer buy?

2. What did the clerk do with the boxed lunch?

3. What size of hot coffee did the customer buy?

Useful Information

［コンビニグルメ］
- corn dog「アメリカンドッグ」　● cream puff「シュークリーム」　● fried potato patty「コロッケ」*
- donut「ドーナツ」　● eclair「エクレア」　● frankfurter「フランクフルトソーセージ」
- fried chicken「鶏の唐揚げ」　● fried chicken skewer「鶏の唐揚げ棒」
- grilled chicken skewer「焼き鳥」　● pudding「プリン」　● steamed meat bun「肉まん」
- steamed sweet bean bun「あんまん」

＊「コロッケ」はフランス語の *croquette* に由来していますが、そのままでは英語話者に通じない場合があります。

Roleplay

Student A スクリプト ▶ p.116

Clerk あなたはコンビニのClerkです。以下の1、3はCustomerから聞いた注文にチェックをつけ、2に個数を記入しましょう。Clerk役を3回行いましょう。

	1	2	3
1st Time	☐ fried chicken ☐ grilled chicken skewer ☐ fried chicken skewer		☐ three large cups for hot coffee ☐ three large cups for cafe latte ☐ three small cups for hot coffee
2nd Time	☐ fried potato patty ☐ steamed meat bun ☐ steamed sweet bean bun		☐ a wet napkin ☐ a spoon ☐ a straw
3rd Time	☐ corn dog ☐ donut ☐ cream puff		☐ two packets of ketchup ☐ two packets of soy sauce ☐ two packets of mustard

Customer 今度はあなたがCustomerです。スクリプトの下線部1〜3に以下の情報を入れてClerkに伝えましょう。Customer役を3回行いましょう。

	1	2	3
1st Time	corn dog	One	one small cup for hot coffee
2nd Time	steamed meat bun	Two	a packet of mustard
3rd Time	grilled chicken skewer	Four	four wet napkins

Roleplay

Student B　スクリプト ▶ p.116

Customer あなたはコンビニのCustomerです。スクリプトの下線部1〜3に以下の情報を入れてClerkに伝えましょう。Customer役を3回行いましょう。

	1	2	3
1st Time	fried chicken skewer	Three	three large cups for cafe latte
2nd Time	steamed sweet bean bun	Two	a straw
3rd Time	donut	Five	two packets of soy sauce

Clerk 今度はあなたがClerkです。以下の1、3はCustomerから聞いた注文にチェックをつけ、2に個数を記入しましょう。Clerk役を3回行いましょう。

	1	2	3
1st Time	☐ donut ☐ corn dog ☐ frankfurter		☐ one small cup for iced coffee ☐ one small cup for hot coffee ☐ one small cup for cafe latte
2nd Time	☐ steamed sweet bean bun ☐ steamed meat bun ☐ grilled chicken skewer		☐ a packet of ketchup ☐ a packet of mustard ☐ a packet of soy sauce
3rd Time	☐ fried chicken ☐ fried chicken skewer ☐ grilled chicken skewer		☐ four forks ☐ four bags ☐ four wet napkins

Reading

 以下のパッセージを読み、質問に英文で答えましょう。

How Convenient Japanese Convenience Stores Can Be!

In big cities, you will see a convenience store on almost every corner. They have been working very hard to meet customers' needs and stay convenient. The average number of items in one convenience store is between 2,500 and 3,000, and most of them are foods. Every convenience store offers *oden*—a popular dish made with various ingredients such as boiled eggs, Japanese radish, and fish cakes stewed in a *dashi* broth. *Oden* is placed near the cashier. You can see the pot and take whatever you like. Convenience stores not only sell goods, but they also offer various services and amenities, such as a clean restroom, sometimes even with a table to change a baby's diaper, a photocopier to send a fax and print out your photos, as well as an ATM. Now, some have even started to deliver boxed lunches and other goods directly to customers' homes or offices. Japanese convenience stores are evolving every day. They are working seriously to be more convenient!

NOTES fish cake「魚肉の練り物」 *dashi* broth「だし」 diaper「おむつ」 evolve「進化する」

1. Why have Japanese convenience stores been working very hard?

2. How many items are there in one convenience store?

3. What is *oden*? Explain it in English.

4. What services or amenities are available? Give two or three examples.

5. What service have they started at some convenience stores?

Special Activity *Oden*

A a～eの英文を並べ替え、コンビニでのおでんの買い方の説明を完成させましょう。

1 (　) → 2 (　) → 3 (　) → 4 (　) → 5 (　)

a. Choose whichever items you like and place them in the container.
b. Pay for your *oden* at the checkout counter. You will be charged by the piece.
c. Select the size of the *oden* container you want at the counter.
d. Use a ladle to add some *dashi* broth.
e. When you pay, you may ask for Japanese mustard.

B 1～8はおでんの具材です。該当する英語をa～hから選びましょう。

1 玉子 (　)

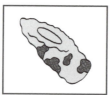
2 ちくわ (　)

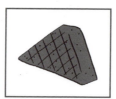
3 こんにゃく (　)

4 昆布 (　)

5 厚揚げ (　)

6 大根 (　)

7 たこ (　)

8 つくね (　)

a. boiled egg　　b. deep-fried tofu　　c. fish meat balls
d. Japanese radish　　e. kelp　　f. octopus
g. tube-shaped fish cake　　h. yam cake

Your total comes to 3,240 yen.

Unit 5

▶ このユニットでは買い物や飲食の会計に関する表現を学びます。

Warm-up

Trial 以下の表現を英語で考えてみましょう。

1. 「お支払いは 3,240 円になります」

2. 「現金かカード、どちらでのお支払いですか」

Useful Words 1〜8の語句の意味をa〜hから選びましょう。また、音声を聞いて発音も確認しましょう。

1. amount (　)　2. change (　)　3. come to (　)　4. PIN (　)
5. receipt (　)　6. return (　)　7. tax (　)　8. within (　)

a. …になる	b. …以内で	c. お釣り	d. 暗証番号
e. 額	f. 税金	g. 返品する	h. 領収書、レシート

1st Dialogue

Dictation レジ係と客の会話を聞き、下線部に単語を記入しましょう。

Cashier: Your ¹._____ comes to 3,240 yen.
Customer: Here.
Cashier: I'll ²._____ 3,240 yen ³._____ of 5,000 yen. 1,760 yen is your ⁴._____. Have a nice day.

Speaking ペアを組んで以下の会話を練習しましょう。Cashierは黒字部分を自由に変えて伝え、Customerはその金額を表に記入しましょう。さまざまなペアで練習を繰り返しましょう。

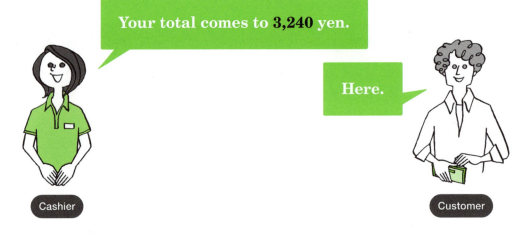

Ex. 3,240

Your total comes to 3,240 yen.

Unit 5

2nd Dialogue

Dictation レジ係と客の会話を聞き、下線部に単語を記入しましょう。

Cashier: 1._____ or credit card?
Customer: Credit card. Here.
Cashier: OK. Please 2._____ your 3._____ here.
Customer: Sure.
Cashier: Thanks. This is your 4._____. Could you check the details?

Speaking ペアを組んで以下の会話を練習しましょう。Customerは黒字部分をCash.かCredit card.のどちらかで答え、Cashierはその回答を○で囲みましょう。さまざまなペアで練習を繰り返しましょう。

Cashier: Cash or credit card?

Customer: Credit card.

Ex.　Cash. / (Credit card.)
　　　Cash. / Credit card.
　　　Cash. / Credit card.
　　　Cash. / Credit card.
　　　Cash. / Credit card.
　　　Cash. / Credit card.
　　　Cash. / Credit card.
　　　Cash. / Credit card.

Listening

 A レジ係と客の会話を聞き、質問に英語で答えましょう。

1. How many items did the customer buy?

2. How much was the change?

3. Within how many days can the customer return goods?

 B レジ係と客の会話を聞き、質問に英語で答えましょう。

1. What was the price?

2. What did the customer enter?

3. What did the customer check last?

Useful Information

[数字の読み方はコンマがポイント]
```
        1 = one
       10 = ten
      100 = one hundred
    1,000 = one thousand
   10,000 = ten thousand
  100,000 = one hundred thousand
1,000,000 = one million
```

Your total comes to 3,240 yen.

Unit 5

Roleplay

Student A スクリプト ▶ p.118

Cashier あなたはCashierです。スクリプトの下線部1〜7に以下の金額や日数を入れてCustomerに伝えましょう。Cashier役を3回行いましょう。

	1	2	3	4	5	6	7
1st Time	520	1,260	970	2,970	3,000	30	14 days
2nd Time	360	13,820	2,650	18,176	20,000	1,824	7 days
3rd Time	1,480	1,800	630	4,222	5,000	778	2 weeks

Customer 今度はあなたがCustomerです。以下の1〜4はCashierから聞いた金額にチェックをつけ、5〜7には金額や日数を記入しましょう。Customer役を3回行いましょう。

	1	2	3	4	5	6	7
1st Time	☐ 630 ☐ 613 ☐ 633	☐ 258 ☐ 2,580 ☐ 2,850	☐ 140 ☐ 401 ☐ 410	☐ 3,199 ☐ 3,919 ☐ 3,909	☐	☐	☐ days
2nd Time	☐ 1,150 ☐ 1,512 ☐ 1,520	☐ 382 ☐ 3,820 ☐ 3,180	☐ 293 ☐ 2,193 ☐ 2,930	☐ 8,913 ☐ 8,930 ☐ 8,931	☐	☐	☐ weeks
3rd Time	☐ 219 ☐ 290 ☐ 299	☐ 1,260 ☐ 12,016 ☐ 12,600	☐ 715 ☐ 750 ☐ 755	☐ 14,173 ☐ 14,713 ☐ 14,731	☐	☐	☐ days

Roleplay

Student B スクリプト ▶ p.118

Customer

あなたはCustomerです。以下の1〜4はCashierから聞いた金額にチェックをつけ、5〜7には金額や日数を記入しましょう。Customer役を3回行いましょう。

	1	2	3	4	5	6	7
1st Time	☐ 512 ☐ 520 ☐ 522	☐ 126 ☐ 1,216 ☐ 1,260	☐ 907 ☐ 917 ☐ 970	☐ 2,097 ☐ 2,917 ☐ 2,970			☐ days
2nd Time	☐ 306 ☐ 316 ☐ 360	☐ 1,382 ☐ 13,180 ☐ 13,820	☐ 265 ☐ 2,650 ☐ 2,065	☐ 18,176 ☐ 8,761 ☐ 18,761			☐ days
3rd Time	☐ 1,080 ☐ 1,418 ☐ 1,480	☐ 108 ☐ 1,800 ☐ 1,810	☐ 603 ☐ 630 ☐ 6,030	☐ 14,222 ☐ 4,222 ☐ 14,422			☐ weeks

Cashier

今度はあなたがCashierです。スクリプトの下線部1〜7に以下の金額や日数を入れてCustomerに伝えましょう。Cashier役を3回行いましょう。

	1	2	3	4	5	6	7
1st Time	630	2,580	410	3,909	5,000	1,091	10 days
2nd Time	1,520	3,820	2,930	8,931	9,000	69	3 weeks
3rd Time	290	12,600	750	14,731	15,000	269	30 days

Reading

以下のパッセージを読み、質問に英文で答えましょう。

Cash, a Tray, and Tape!

There are a few tips that may help you when shopping in Japan. First, Japan is a cash society. In your country, you may go to the supermarket and get only chewing gum and pay by credit card. It is not very common in Japan. Some small shops in Japan do not even accept credit cards. So, it is always wise to carry enough cash with you. Next, when paying in Japan, you usually do not give cash to a cashier directly. There is a tray on the counter, and you are expected to put the money there. By doing so, it is clear how much money you have paid, and prevents trouble. Finally, if you do not need a plastic shopping bag, you will be asked if it is okay to put tape on your purchases. This tape is proof that you paid. In some stores, they will put tape on every single item that is not in a bag!

NOTES prevent「防止する」 proof「証明」

1. What is not common in Japan?

2. Why is it wise to carry enough cash with you in Japan?

3. What do you usually not give to a cashier directly?

4. Why do people put the money on a tray?

5. Why does a cashier put the tape on your purchases?

Special Activity: Sign

 看板や貼り紙に記されているNoは「禁止、厳禁、不可」を、Onlyは「専用」を意味します。1〜12の表現を日本語にしてみましょう。

No Littering
ポイ捨て禁止

Women Only
女性専用

1 No Smoking　　　　　　＿＿＿＿＿＿＿＿＿＿
2 No Parking　　　　　　 ＿＿＿＿＿＿＿＿＿＿
3 No Shoes　　　　　　　＿＿＿＿＿＿＿＿＿＿
4 No Photography　　　　＿＿＿＿＿＿＿＿＿＿
5 No Cell Phones　　　　 ＿＿＿＿＿＿＿＿＿＿
6 No Food or Drinks　　　＿＿＿＿＿＿＿＿＿＿

7 Burnable Trash Only　　＿＿＿＿＿＿＿＿＿＿
8 Employees Only　　　　＿＿＿＿＿＿＿＿＿＿
9 Exit Only　　　　　　　＿＿＿＿＿＿＿＿＿＿
10 Entry Only　　　　　　＿＿＿＿＿＿＿＿＿＿
11 Pedestrians Only　　　 ＿＿＿＿＿＿＿＿＿＿
12 Guests Only　　　　　 ＿＿＿＿＿＿＿＿＿＿

B 1〜12の表現から4つを選び、イラスト入りの貼り紙を作ってみましょう。

Unit 6 I'm truly sorry for the trouble.

▶ このユニットでは商品やサービスへの苦情とその対応に関する表現を学びます。

Warm-up

Trial 以下の表現を英語で考えてみましょう。

1.「ご迷惑をおかけして申し訳ございません」

_____

2.「他のものがあるか確認いたします」

_____

Useful Words 1〜8の語句の意味をa〜hから選びましょう。また、音声を聞いて発音も確認しましょう。 🎧 36

1. apologize ( )　　**2.** come back in stock ( )　　**3.** exchange ( )

4. free of charge ( )　　**5.** get a refund ( )　　**6.** inconvenience ( )

7. out of stock ( )　　**8.** wrong ( )

a. お詫びする	**b.** 間違いの	**c.** 交換する	**d.** 再入荷される
e. 品切れ	**f.** 不便	**g.** 払い戻しを受ける	**h.** 無料で

49

1st Dialogue

Dictation 客とレストランのホールスタッフの会話を聞き、下線部に単語を記入しましょう。 37

Guest: ^{1.}_____ me.
Server: Yes? Can I help you?
Guest: There is a hair in my ^{2.}_____.
Server: I'm ^{3.}_____ sorry for the ^{4.}_____. I'll ^{5.}_____ you a new one now.

Speaking ペアを組んで以下の会話を練習しましょう。Guestは黒字部分を枠内の語句と入れ替えて伝え、Serverはその内容を表に記入しましょう。さまざまなペアで練習を繰り返しましょう。

Guest: Excuse me. There is **a hair** in my food.

Server: I'm truly sorry for the trouble.

Ex. *a hair*

a hair
a bug
something
some dirt
a rubber band
some plastic

Unit 6

I'm truly sorry for the trouble.

2nd Dialogue

Dictation 客と販売員の会話を聞き、下線部に単語を記入しましょう。

Customer: Hi. I bought this yesterday. This is 1._____.

Clerk: Oh, I 2._____ for the 3._____. Let me 4._____ if we have another one.

Speaking ペアを組んで以下の会話を練習しましょう。Customerは黒字部分を枠内の語句と入れ替えて伝え、Clerkはその内容を表に記入しましょう。さまざまなペアで練習を繰り返しましょう。

Customer: Excuse me, this is **broken**.

Clerk: Oh, I apologize for the inconvenience.

Ex. broken

- broken
- torn
- dirty
- chipped
- loose
- scratched

Listening

A 客とレストランのホールスタッフの会話を聞きましょう。設問1、2は下線部に単語を記入して答えを完成させ、3は質問に英語で答えましょう。

1. What is the problem with the food?

   The server brought the _____ food.

2. How does the server respond to the problem?

   They will _____ a new one.

3. What will the server bring free of charge?

   _____

B 客と販売員の会話を聞きましょう。設問1は質問に英語で答え、2、3は下線部に単語を記入して答えを完成させましょう。

1. When did the customer buy the item?

   _____

2. What is the problem with the item?

   It is the wrong _____.

3. Why did the customer ask for a refund?

   Because the item is _____ _____ _____ now.

Useful Information

[購入品の問題点を伝える表現]
- This is (broken / chipped / cracked / dented / dirty / loose / scratched / torn).
  「これは (壊れて / 欠けて / ひびが入って / へこんで / 汚れて / ほつれて / 傷がついて / 破れて) います」
- This is the wrong (color / item / kind / size / style).
  「これは (色 / 商品 / 種類 / サイズ / 型) が間違っています」

Roleplay

Student A スクリプト ▶ p.118

Customer あなたはCustomerです。スクリプトの下線部1に以下の問題点を入れてClerkに伝え、2はClerkから聞いた情報にチェックをつけましょう。Customer役を3回行いましょう。

	1	2
1st Time	torn	☐ next Monday ☐ next Tuesday ☐ next Wednesday
2nd Time	the wrong color	☐ in a few days ☐ in a week ☐ in two weeks
3rd Time	chipped	☐ this afternoon ☐ tomorrow ☐ the day after tomorrow

Clerk 今度はあなたがClerkです。スクリプトの下線部2に以下の情報を入れてCustomerに伝え、1はCustomerから聞いた問題点にチェックをつけましょう。Clerk役を3回行いましょう。

	1	2
1st Time	☐ broken ☐ dented ☐ dirty	this weekend
2nd Time	☐ the wrong color ☐ the wrong item ☐ the wrong style	in a few days
3rd Time	☐ broken ☐ cracked ☐ scratched	tomorrow

I'm truly sorry for the trouble. Unit 6

Roleplay

Student B スクリプト ▶ p.118

Clerk あなたはClerkです。スクリプトの下線部2に以下の情報を入れてCustomerに伝え、1はCustomerから聞いた問題点にチェックをつけましょう。Clerk役を3回行いましょう。

	1	2
1st Time	☐ cracked ☐ loose ☐ torn	next Wednesday
2nd Time	☐ the wrong color ☐ the wrong kind ☐ the wrong size	in a week
3rd Time	☐ broken ☐ chipped ☐ dented	the day after tomorrow

Customer 今度はあなたがCustomerです。スクリプトの下線部1に以下の問題点を入れてClerkに伝え、2はClerkから聞いた情報にチェックをつけましょう。Customer役を3回行いましょう。

	1	2
1st Time	dirty	☐ this week ☐ this weekend ☐ next week
2nd Time	the wrong item	☐ in a few hours ☐ in a few days ☐ in a few weeks
3rd Time	broken	☐ this afternoon ☐ tomorrow ☐ the day after tomorrow

Reading

▼ 以下のパッセージを読み、質問に英文で答えましょう。

Very Polite Service Staff Who Love Manuals

Have you heard the word *omotenashi*? It means thoughtful and dedicated hospitality given to customers. It is difficult to translate into simple English, but the idea is that service staff do their very best to meet your wants and needs in order for you to enjoy your time, without really expecting anything in return. During your visit to Japan, you may feel very special because you will most likely be treated very politely. As *omotenashi* is important for service staff, Japanese people heavily rely on manuals. Most service industry businesses have huge manuals or guides. For example, you order a *tempura* lunch that comes with a bowl of *miso* soup, and you want to change the *miso* soup to a different soup on the menu. It may seem a very simple and reasonable request, especially where *omotenashi* is practiced. However, the server may very politely refuse your request if changing *miso* soup to something else is not in the manual.

NOTES ▶ dedicated「献身的な」 in return「お返しに」 rely on「…に頼る」

1. Why do service staff do their very best?

2. Why would tourists feel very special during their visit to Japan?

3. What do Japanese people in the service industry heavily rely on?

4. According to the example, what is the tourist's request?

5. Why may the server refuse the tourist's request?

Special Activity — Apology

A 下線部に適語を入れて、お詫びやお知らせの表現を完成させましょう。

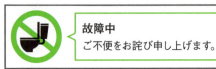

1 _____
_____ Out
Coming Back in _____ Soon

2 Out of _____
Sorry for the _____

B 1〜4の客の苦情に対する適切な応答をa〜dから選び、店員の吹き出しの中に記入しましょう。

a. I'm very sorry, ma'am. I'll check with the kitchen.
b. I'm terribly sorry, sir. I'll bring a new one.
c. I'm truly sorry. I'll bring a new glass.
d. I apologize for the trouble. I'll clean the table right away.

Review 1   Units 1–6

Key Vocabulary

A 1〜12の語句の意味をa〜lから選びましょう。

1. apologize   (　　)   7. meal   (　　)
2. available   (　　)   8. order   (　　)
3. change   (　　)   9. PIN   (　　)
4. come with   (　　)   10. refill   (　　)
5. get a refund (　　)   11. reservation (　　)
6. heat up   (　　)   12. separate   (　　)

a. …についてくる	b. お釣り	c. 温める	d. お代わり
e. お詫びする	f. 暗証番号	g. 食事	h. 注文する
i. 分ける	j. 払い戻しを受ける	k. 予約	l. 利用できる、空いている

B 英語は日本語に、日本語は英語にしましょう。

1. buckwheat noodles   → _____
2. hot towel   → _____
3. oolong tea   → _____
4. steamed sweet bean bun   → _____
5. 青ねぎ   → _____
6. ごまドレッシング   → _____
7. しょうゆ   → _____
8. 弁当   → _____

Key Expressions

A [ ] 内の語句を並べ替え、以下の表現を英語にしましょう。ただし不足している1語は自分で追加し、文頭の単語は大文字で始めましょう。

1. 「ご注文はお決まりでしょうか」
   [are / order / to / you / ?]

2. 「まず始めにお飲み物はいかがでしょうか」
   [some drinks / like / to / with / would / you / ?]

3. 「こちらは魚貝類と野菜用のつゆでございます」
   [and / for / is / seafood / the / this / vegetables / .]

4. 「お箸はいくつご入用ですか」
   [do / how / need / many / you / ?]

5. 「お支払いは 3,240 円になります」
   [comes / 3,240 yen / to / your / .]

6. 「他のものがあるか確認いたします」
   [check / if / have / let / me / one / we / .]

B 1～6の英文を聞き、それぞれの応答として最も適切なものをa～hから選びましょう。 🎧43

1. (　)　2. (　)　3. (　)　4. (　)　5. (　)　6. (　)

- **a.** Credit card.
- **b.** Five.
- **c.** I enjoyed the party.
- **d.** I'm truly sorry for the trouble.
- **e.** Sure. I'll be right back.
- **f.** To go, please.
- **g.** Very good.
- **h.** Yes, please.

Listening

A レストランのホールスタッフと客の会話を聞き、質問に英語で答えましょう。 🎧44

1. What did the guest order?

2. What are the two things the guest may have with the *tempura*?

3. What will the server bring?

B コンビニの店員と客の会話を聞き、質問に英語で答えましょう。 🎧45

1. How many steamed meat buns did the customer buy?

2. How much did the customer pay?

3. What did the customer enter?

Reading

▼ 次の英文を読み、Units 1〜6のパッセージの内容と一致する場合はT、一致しない場合はFを○で囲みましょう。

1. *Ekiben* were first created for small children. [T / F]
2. There are recipe books for *kyaraben*. [T / F]
3. *Kaitenzushi* means sushi at a baggage claim. [T / F]
4. At a *kaitenzushi* restaurant, you may return empty plates to the belt. [T / F]
5. You should clink glasses with everyone in an *izakaya*. [T / F]
6. Japanese people usually pour drinks for others. [T / F]
7. Most of the items sold in a convenience store in Japan are foods. [T / F]
8. Japanese convenience stores are evolving every day. [T / F]
9. It is not necessary to carry cash with you in Japan. [T / F]
10. You should give money to a cashier directly when paying in Japan. [T / F]
11. *Omotenashi* is thoughtful and dedicated hospitality given to customers. [T / F]
12. Service staff in Japan heavily rely on manuals or guides. [T / F]

Do you have a reservation?

Unit 7

▶ このユニットではホテルや旅館での宿泊客受付に関する表現を学びます。

Warm-up

Trial 以下の表現を英語で考えてみましょう。

1.「ご予約はいただいておりますか」

2.「こちらの用紙に記入していただけますか」

Useful Words 1〜8の語句の意味をa〜hから選びましょう。また、音声を聞いて発音も確認しましょう。

1. check in (　)　2. electricity (　)　3. I'm afraid (　)　4. in advance (　)
5. insert (　)　6. prefer (　)　7. reserve (　)　8. turn on (　)

a. …のほうを好む　b. …を作動させる　c. チェックインする　d. 恐縮ですが
e. 差し込む　f. 前もって　g. 電気　h. 予約する

1st Dialogue

Dictation ホテルのフロント係と客の会話を聞き、下線部に単語を記入しましょう。

Desk Clerk: Hello, sir. May I ¹._____ you?

Guest: Yes. I'm ²._____ _____.

Desk Clerk: Do you have a ³._____?

Guest: Yes. I'm Tim Davis.

Speaking ペアを組んで以下の会話を練習しましょう。Guestは黒字部分を自分の名前に入れ替えて伝え、Desk Clerkはその名前を表に記入しましょう。さまざまなペアで練習を繰り返しましょう。

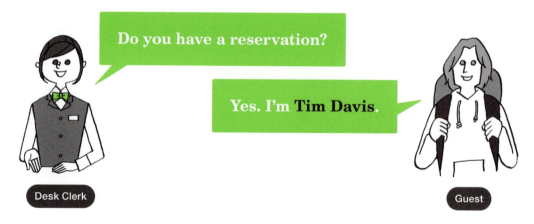

Ex. *Tim Davis*

Unit 7 — Do you have a reservation?

2nd Dialogue

Dictation 1st Dialogueの続きを聞き、下線部に単語を記入しましょう。

Desk Clerk: Could you fill out this ¹_____?
Guest: Sure.
Desk Clerk: How would you like to ²_____? ³_____ or credit card?
Guest: Credit card, please.
Desk Clerk: May I ⁴_____ your card, please?
Guest: Here.

Speaking ペアを組んで以下の会話を練習しましょう。Desk Clerkは自分のテキストを記入用紙として差し出し、Guestはそのテキストの表に自分の名前を記入しましょう。さまざまなペアで練習を繰り返しましょう。

Ex. *Tim Davis*

Listening

A ホテルのフロント係と客の会話を聞き、質問に英語で答えましょう。

1. What type of room did the guest reserve?

2. How long will the guest stay?

3. What type of room does the guest want?

B Ⓐの会話の続きを聞きましょう。設問1、2は質問に英語で答え、3は下線部に単語を記入して答えを完成させましょう。

1. How did the guest pay?

2. What did the desk clerk give the guest when he returned her credit card?

3. What should the guest do to turn on all the electricity in the room?

   She should _____ her _____ card in the slot near the _____.

Useful Information

[宿泊施設の部屋の種類]
- (single / double / twin) room「(シングル / ダブル / ツイン) ルーム」
- (smoking / non-smoking) room「(喫煙 / 禁煙) ルーム」
- room with a (king-size / queen-size) bed「(キングサイズ / クィーンサイズ) ベッドがある部屋」
- room with (an ocean / a mountain / a river / a city) view「(海 / 山 / 川 / 街) の見える部屋」
- room by the (elevator / entrance)「(エレベーター / 入口) に近い部屋」
- room on a (high / low) floor「(高層階 / 低層階) の部屋」
- Western-style room with (breakfast / dinner / two meals)「(朝食 / 夕食 / 2食) つきの洋室」
- Japanese-style room with an open-air bath「露天風呂つきの和室」

Roleplay

Student A スクリプト ▶ p.120

Desk Clerk あなたはホテルのDesk Clerkです。スクリプトの下線部2～4に以下の情報を入れてGuestに確認し、5はGuestから聞いた情報にチェックをつけましょう。Desk Clerk役を3回行いましょう。

	2	3	4	5
1st Time	Mr. Rowan	single	two nights	☐ room with a queen-size bed ☐ room with an open-air bath ☐ room with a king-size bed
2nd Time	Ms. Walker	double	four nights	☐ smoking room ☐ room by the elevator ☐ non-smoking room
3rd Time	Mr. Brown	twin	three nights	☐ room with a city view ☐ room with an ocean view ☐ room with a mountain view

Guest 今度はあなたがGuestです。スクリプトの下線部1、5に以下の情報を入れてDesk Clerkに伝えましょう。Guest役を3回行いましょう。

	1	5
1st Time	Vicky White	smoking room
2nd Time	David Adams	Western-style room with breakfast
3rd Time	Monica Smith	room on a high floor

Roleplay

Student B スクリプト ▶ p.120

Guest あなたはホテルのGuestです。スクリプトの下線部1、5に以下の情報を入れてDesk Clerkに伝えましょう。Guest役を3回行いましょう。

	1	5
1st Time	Brian Rowan	room with a king-size bed
2nd Time	Cathy Walker	non-smoking room
3rd Time	Eric Brown	room with an ocean view

Desk Clerk 今度はあなたがDesk Clerkです。スクリプトの下線部2〜4に以下の情報を入れてGuestに確認し、5はGuestから聞いた情報にチェックをつけましょう。Desk Clerk役を3回行いましょう。

	2	3	4	5
1st Time	Ms. White	twin	three nights	☐ smoking room ☐ room with an open-air bath ☐ non-smoking room
2nd Time	Mr. Adams	double	one night	☐ Western-style room with two meals ☐ Japanese-style room with dinner ☐ Western-style room with breakfast
3rd Time	Ms. Smith	single	two nights	☐ room with a river view ☐ room by the entrance ☐ room on a high floor

Reading

▼ 以下のパッセージを読み、質問に英文で答えましょう。

No Clothes Necessary

Going to a hot spring, *onsen* in Japanese, is becoming very popular among foreign tourists, and has been ranked first as an activity they would want to do again. You should also try visiting an *onsen*. There are some rules you should know about bathing in an *onsen*. Though it is common for people to wear swimsuits when they use a hot tub or Jacuzzi in many other countries, one important rule in Japan is that you need to remove all your clothes when bathing in a hot spring or public bath. You may have heard that Japanese are shy; however, after bathing in a Japanese *onsen*, you begin to think differently. You can even try bathing without a swimsuit in an open-air bath looking at the beautiful sky. You may be so relaxed that you will want to do it again. When in Japan, do as the Japanese people do. This is essential for you to fully enjoy a hot spring in Japan!

NOTES ▶ bathe「入浴する」 Jacuzzi「ジャグジー」 essential「不可欠の」

1. How do you say "*onsen*" in English?

2. What would foreign tourists want to do again?

3. In many other countries, what do people usually wear in a hot tub or Jacuzzi?

4. Before bathing in a Japanese *onsen*, what may people think about Japanese?

5. What is essential for you to fully enjoy a hot spring in Japan?

Special Activity: Japanese Inn

 A ①〜⑧は旅館でよく見かけるものです。それぞれの説明をa〜hから選んで線で結びましょう。

① 下駄
② 畳
③ 押入れ
④ 障子
⑤ 床の間
⑥ 掛け軸
⑦ 浴衣
⑧ ふすま

a. alcove
b. casual summer kimono
c. closet for futon storage
d. decorative hanging scroll
e. sliding paper door made of thick paper
f. sliding paper screen used like a curtain on the window
g. traditional straw flooring
h. traditional wooden footwear

 B a〜dの英文を並べ替え、日本茶のいれ方の説明を完成させましょう。

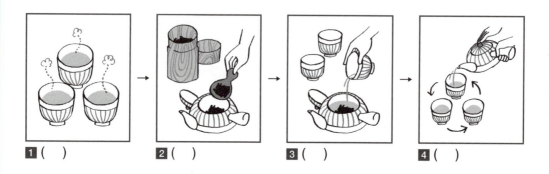

① (　)　② (　)　③ (　)　④ (　)

a. Pour the tea from the tea pot, little by little, moving between the cups like the picture shows.
b. Put some hot water in cups and let it cool a little.
c. From the tea container, scoop about one heaping teaspoon of tea leaves per person, and then put them in the tea pot.
d. Put the hot water from the cups into the tea pot, and wait for about a minute to let the tea steep.

Wi-Fi is available in this area.

Unit 8

▶ このユニットでは客が利用できるサービスや近隣情報の案内に関する表現を学びます。

Warm-up

Trial 以下の表現を英語で考えてみましょう。

1. 「Wi-Fi はこちらのエリアでご利用可能です」

_____

2. 「恐縮ですが、コピー機はございません」

_____

Useful Words 1〜8の語句の意味をa〜hから選びましょう。また、音声を聞いて発音も確認しましょう。

1. across from (　)　　2. behind (　)　　3. in front of (　)
4. look for (　)　　5. next to (　)　　6. specialty (　)
7. typical (　)　　8. whole building (　)

> a. …の後ろに　　b. …の向かいに　　c. …の前に　　d. …の隣に
> e. …を探す　　f. 建物全体　　g. 代表的な　　h. 名産品

1st Dialogue

Dictation 客とカフェの店員の会話を聞き、下線部に単語を記入しましょう。

Customer: Excuse me. Is there a Wi-Fi ¹._____ here?
Clerk: Yes. It's ²._____ in this area.
Customer: OK.
Clerk: Just use this ³._____ and ⁴._____.

Speaking ペアを組んで以下の会話を練習しましょう。Clerkは黒字部分を枠内の語句と入れ替えて伝え、Customerはその内容を表に記入しましょう。さまざまなペアで練習を繰り返しましょう。

Excuse me. Is there a Wi-Fi connection here?

Yes. It's available **in this area**.

Ex. *in this area*

in this area
in the customer seating area
in the whole building
on the second floor
in the lobby

Wi-Fi is available in this area.

2nd Dialogue

Dictation ホテルのフロント係と客の会話を聞き、下線部に単語を記入しましょう。 55

Desk Clerk: Hello, can I help you?

Guest: Hi. Do you have a copy ^{1.}_____?

Desk Clerk: I'm ^{2.}_____ we don't. There is a ^{3.}_____ store ^{4.}_____ to the hotel.

Guest: OK, thanks.

Speaking ペアを組んで以下の会話を練習しましょう。Guestは黒字部分を枠内の語句と入れ替えて質問し、Desk Clerkはその内容を表に記入しましょう。さまざまなペアで練習を繰り返しましょう。

Hi. Do you have **a copy machine**?

I'm afraid we don't.

Guest

Desk Clerk

Ex. *a copy machine*

a copy machine
a souvenir shop
a laundromat
a coffee shop
a swimming pool
an ATM

Listening

A カフェの店員と客の会話を聞きましょう。設問1、2は質問に英語で答え、3は下線部に単語を記入して答えを完成させましょう。 🎧 56

1. Who can use a Wi-Fi connection?
   _____

2. What should the customer type to access the Internet?
   _____

3. Where is the restroom?

   Outside of the _____, on the _____.

B ホテルのフロント係と客の会話を聞き、質問に英語で答えましょう。 🎧 57

1. What did the guest want?
   _____

2. Where is the drugstore?
   _____

3. What is the specialty of the area?
   _____

Useful Information 🎧 58

[さまざまな日本のお土産]
- citrus cookie「ゆずクッキー」 ● good-luck charm「お守り」
- green tea cookie「抹茶クッキー」 ● indigo-dyed handkerchief「藍染のハンカチ」
- Japanese fan「扇子」 ● *kanji* keychain「漢字のキーホルダー」 ● pottery dish「陶器」
- rice cake「もち」 ● rice cracker「せんべい」 ● steamed bun「まんじゅう」
- washcloth「手ぬぐい」 ● wooden chopsticks「木製の箸」 ● wrapping cloth「風呂敷」

Wi-Fi is available in this area.

Unit 8

Roleplay

Student A　スクリプト ▶ p.120

Desk Clerk　あなたはホテルのDesk Clerkです。スクリプトの下線部2、3に以下の情報を入れてGuestに伝え、1はGuestからの質問内容にチェックをつけましょう。Desk Clerk役を3回行いましょう。

	1	2	3
1st Time	☐ a cafe ☐ a restaurant ☐ room service	a restaurant across from the hotel	green tea cookies
2nd Time	☐ a hot spring ☐ a swimming pool ☐ a Jacuzzi	a gym next to the station	rice crackers
3rd Time	☐ a coffee maker ☐ a copy machine ☐ a souvenir shop	a convenience store behind the hotel	handmade Japanese fans

Guest　今度はあなたがGuestです。スクリプトの下線部1に以下の質問内容を入れてDesk Clerkに尋ね、2、3はDesk Clerkから聞いた情報にチェックをつけましょう。Guest役を3回行いましょう。

	1	2	3
1st Time	a shuttle bus	☐ a bus stop in front of the hotel ☐ an express bus at the station ☐ an express train at the station	☐ rice cakes ☐ wrapping cloths ☐ wooden chopsticks
2nd Time	a souvenir shop	☐ a gift shop in front of the station ☐ a souvenir shop behind the hotel ☐ a gift shop near the station	☐ citrus cookies ☐ green tea cookies ☐ steamed buns
3rd Time	an ATM	☐ a bank behind the hotel ☐ a bank next to the hotel ☐ a bank in front of the hotel	☐ good-luck charms ☐ *kanji* keychains ☐ pottery dishes

Roleplay

Student B スクリプト ▶ p.120

Guest あなたはホテルのGuestです。スクリプトの下線部1に以下の質問内容を入れてDesk Clerkに尋ね、2、3はDesk Clerkから聞いた情報にチェックをつけましょう。Guest役を3回行いましょう。

	1	2	3
1st Time	room service	☐ a cafe across from the hotel ☐ a restaurant across from the hotel ☐ a restaurant next to the hotel	☐ good-luck charms ☐ citrus cookies ☐ green tea cookies
2nd Time	a swimming pool	☐ a gym next to the station ☐ a gym in front of the station ☐ a gym next to the hotel	☐ rice crackers ☐ rice cakes ☐ wrapping cloths
3rd Time	a copy machine	☐ a convenience store near the hotel ☐ a convenience store near here ☐ a convenience store behind the hotel	☐ indigo-dyed handkerchiefs ☐ handmade Japanese fans ☐ washcloths

Desk Clerk 今度はあなたがDesk Clerkです。スクリプトの下線部2、3に以下の情報を入れてGuestに伝え、1はGuestからの質問内容にチェックをつけましょう。Desk Clerk役を3回行いましょう。

	1	2	3
1st Time	a limousine a shuttle bus a rent-a-car	an express train at the station	wooden chopsticks
2nd Time	a gift shop a coffee shop a souvenir shop	a gift shop in front of the station	citrus cookies
3rd Time	an ATM a convenience store a vending machine	a bank next to the hotel	pottery dishes

Reading

 以下のパッセージを読み、質問に英文で答えましょう。

Experience High-Tech Toilets

Japanese toilets are very high-tech compared to other countries'. They have many unique functions that make your time in the restroom comfortable. This is how it works: when you enter an individual stall, the toilet lid opens automatically. Sitting there, you will be surprised to see a panel with many buttons on the wall. It has many functions. The temperature of the seat can be adjusted, so it is quite comfortable to sit on. There is even a button to make a fake flushing sound. This was invented as some Japanese people do not want to be heard by other people. Finally, there is a button to spray water in order to clean yourself. When you stand up, some toilets flush automatically, or they flush by putting your hand over a sensor. What may surprise you even more is that these restrooms are free, and you can find them in almost all public places. Moreover, about 75% of Japanese homes have high-tech toilets, too.

NOTES　stall「小部屋、個室」　lid「ふた」　automatically「自動的に」　temperature「温度」　adjust「調節する」　quite「かなり」　flush「流す」

1. When you enter an individual stall, what will happen?

2. Why is it quite comfortable to sit on the seat?

3. Why was a fake flushing sound invented?

4. How can you flush the toilet when it does not flush automatically?

5. Where can you find these toilets? Give two examples.

Special Activity: Souvenir

A 日本のお土産として購入されることが多い「漢字Tシャツ」の漢字を英語にしてみましょう。

1. 侍 _____
2. 一番 _____
3. 幸 _____
4. 夢 _____
5. 魂 _____
6. 正義 _____
7. 愛 _____
8. 福 _____
9. 祭 _____
10. 神 _____

B 1～6は外国人旅行者に人気のお土産です。それぞれの説明をa～fから選びましょう。

1. chopsticks ( )
2. Japanese pens ( )
3. Hello Kitty goods ( )
4. personal seals ( )
5. plastic wrap for food ( )
6. Japanese snacks ( )

a. People like them very much because they simply taste good. Japanese and Western flavor combinations are popular.

b. These are very traditional souvenirs, and people sometimes use them as hair accessories.

c. They do not cut as easily as the ones in Japan, and in some countries, they do not even have a cutter.

d. They have various colors, sizes, and functions. They are smooth, durable, and are reasonably priced.

e. You can create them with your name or favorite words in *hiragana*, *katakana* or *kanji*.

f. If you love this world-famous character, Japan is the best place to get the limited products.

I highly recommend Sakura Restaurant. Unit 9

▶ このユニットでは旅行者の希望に応じた店や観光地などの提案に関する表現を学びます。

Warm-up

Trial 以下の表現を英語で考えてみましょう。

1. 「桜レストランが大変お勧めです」
___

2. 「ここから徒歩で5分のところに美しいお寺がありますよ」
___

Useful Words 1～8の語句の意味をa～hから選びましょう。また、音声を聞いて発音も確認しましょう。

1. allergy (　)　　2. brochure (　)　　3. budget (　)
4. reasonable (　)　　5. recommend (　)　　6. shrine (　)
7. sightseeing spot (　)　　8. temple (　)

> a. 勧める　　b. アレルギー　　c. 観光スポット　　d. 冊子、パンフレット
> e. 手頃な　　f. 寺　　g. 神社　　h. 予算

1st Dialogue

Dictation 旅行者と観光ボランティアの会話を聞き、下線部に単語を記入しましょう。

Tourist: Hi. Is there a nice Japanese restaurant around here?
Volunteer: What's your ¹._____?
Tourist: About 1,000 yen ²._____ _____.
Volunteer: Then, I ³._____ _____ Sakura Restaurant.

Speaking ペアを組んで以下の会話を練習しましょう。Touristは黒字部分を自由に変えて伝え、Volunteerはその金額を表に記入しましょう。さまざまなペアで練習を繰り返しましょう。

What's your budget?

About **1,000** yen per person.

Then, I highly recommend Sakura Restaurant.

Volunteer

Tourist

Ex. *1,000*

Unit 9

I highly recommend Sakura Restaurant.

2nd Dialogue

Dictation 旅行者と観光ボランティアの会話を聞き、下線部に単語を記入しましょう。

Tourist: Hi. We'd like to ¹._____ something Japanese. Are there any ²._____ _____ around here?

Volunteer: Sure. There is a beautiful temple just a five-minute ³._____ from here.

Tourist: Sounds great.

Speaking ペアを組んで以下の会話を練習しましょう。Volunteerは黒字部分を枠内の語句と入れ替えて伝え、Touristはその内容を表に記入しましょう。さまざまなペアで練習を繰り返しましょう。

Tourist: Are there any sightseeing spots around here?

Volunteer: Sure. There is a beautiful **temple** just a five-minute walk from here.

Ex. *temple*

temple
shrine
Japanese garden
castle
tower
park
fountain

79

Listening

 A 旅行者と観光ボランティアの会話を聞き、質問に英語で答えましょう。

1. What kind of food are the tourists interested in?

2. What is the tourists' budget?

3. What is the name of the restaurant the tourists will probably go to?

 B 観光ボランティアと旅行者の会話を聞き、質問に英語で答えましょう。

1. How far away is the famous shrine?

2. Where are the tourists most likely to go?

3. What did the volunteer give to the tourists?

Useful Information

［和食店の定番メニュー］
- buckwheat noodles「そば」　● deep-fried pork「とんかつ」
- grilled chicken skewer「焼き鳥」　● grilled eel「うなぎの蒲焼」
- Japanese-style pizza「お好み焼き」　● thick wheat noodles「うどん」

［店や料理の特徴］
- casual「カジュアルな、敷居が低い」　● delicious「おいしい」　● famous「有名な」
- high-quality「質が高い、高級な」　● nice「素敵な、雰囲気が良い」　● popular「人気がある」
- reasonable「手頃な料金の」　● tasty「おいしい、風味がある」　● traditional「伝統的な」

Unit 9

I highly recommend Sakura Restaurant.

Roleplay

Student A スクリプト ▶ p.122

Tourist あなたはTouristです。スクリプトの下線部1に以下の金額を入れてVolunteerに伝え、2〜5はVolunteerから聞いた情報にチェックをつけましょう。Tourist役を3回行いましょう。

	1	2	3	4	5
1st Time	3,000	☐ tasty ☐ famous ☐ nice	☐ *yakiniku* ☐ *yakiton* ☐ *tonkatsu*	☐ Yoshi ☐ Bushi ☐ Kishi	☐ grilled meat ☐ grilled pork ☐ deep-fried pork
2nd Time	2,500	☐ delicious ☐ popular ☐ tasty	☐ *yakiton* ☐ *okonomiyaki* ☐ *yakitori*	☐ Tomo ☐ Toyo ☐ Tono	☐ grilled chicken ☐ grilled pork ☐ Japanese-style pizza
3rd Time	2,000	☐ famous ☐ casual ☐ popular	☐ *domburi* ☐ *udon* ☐ *okonomiyaki*	☐ Tsuki ☐ Sachi ☐ Michi	☐ thick wheat noodles ☐ Japanese-style pizza ☐ rice bowl

Volunteer 今度はあなたがVolunteerです。スクリプトの下線部2〜5に以下の情報を入れてTouristに伝え、1にはTouristから聞いた金額を記入しましょう。Volunteer役を3回行いましょう。

	1	2	3	4	5
1st Time		popular	*unagi*	Nakaya	grilled eel
2nd Time		reasonable	*udon*	Tsukimi	thick wheat noodles
3rd Time		tasty	*domburi*	Dondon	rice bowl

Roleplay

Student B スクリプト ▶ p.122

Volunteer あなたはVolunteerです。スクリプトの下線部2〜5に以下の情報を入れてTouristに伝え、1にはTouristから聞いた金額を記入しましょう。Volunteer役を3回行いましょう。

	1	2	3	4	5
1st Time		famous	*tonkatsu*	Yoshi	deep-fried pork
2nd Time		delicious	*yakitori*	Toyo	grilled chicken
3rd Time		casual	*okonomiyaki*	Michi	Japanese-style pizza

Tourist 今度はあなたがTouristです。スクリプトの下線部1に以下の金額を入れてVolunteerに伝え、2〜5はVolunteerから聞いた情報にチェックをつけましょう。Tourist役を3回行いましょう。

	1	2	3	4	5
1st Time	3,500	traditional high-quality popular	*yakiniku* *unagi* *tonkatsu*	Sakaya Nakaya Takaya	grilled eel deep-fried pork grilled meat
2nd Time	1,000	reasonable nice casual	*yakiton* *udon* *yakitori*	Kitsune Tsukimi Tanuki	grilled pork grilled chicken thick wheat noodles
3rd Time	2,000	famous tasty delicious	*tonkatsu* *udon* *domburi*	Dondon Tantan Tenten	rice bowl deep-fried pork thick wheat noodles

Reading

 以下のパッセージを読み、質問に英文で答えましょう。

Finding Peace of Mind on Mt. Koya

Do you want to experience something spiritual you can only do in Japan? Then, a temple stay on Mt. Koya, a Buddhist sanctuary, is highly recommended. Temple lodgings, or *shukubo*, limited to only monks in the past, are now very popular among tourists. Monks will help you by serving vegetarian meals and putting out your futon. You can also attend a morning ceremony which starts before breakfast. Some temples offer *goma* fire rituals. There are also other religious experiences you can try, for example, hand-copying a Buddhist sutra, or *shakyo*. While you are hand-copying, you are supposed to make one wish to keep a pure mind. You can even participate in a meditation class, called *ajikan*. The monks will teach you how to sit and breathe, so that you will be very relaxed and peaceful. You should feel very calm and at ease after these experiences. If you are looking for something truly Japanese and something spiritual, you should definitely try Mt. Koya!

NOTES Buddhist「仏教の」 sanctuary「神聖な場所」 lodging「宿泊」 monk「僧」 put out「…を出す」 ritual「儀式」 sutra「お経」 meditation「瞑想」

1. What is highly recommended?

2. Who were allowed to stay in *shukubo* before?

3. What will monks help you with?

4. What kinds of religious experiences can you try there? Give more than two examples.

5. How would a tourist feel after the experiences?

Special Activity — Culture

1 ～ 12 は日本文化を体験するためのアクティビティです。それぞれの説明をa～lから選びましょう。

1 華道（　）

2 芸者体験（　）

3 書道（　）

4 はた織り（　）

5 食品サンプル作り（　）

6 折り紙（　）

7 座禅（　）

8 茶道（　）

9 陶芸（　）

10 忍者体験（　）

11 盆栽（　）

12 和紙作り（　）

a. calligraphy　**b.** flower arrangement　**c.** food replica crafting
d. *geisha* makeover　**e.** seated meditation　**f.** miniature tree cultivation
g. *ninja* experience　**h.** paper folding　**i.** pottery making
j. tea ceremony　**k.** traditional paper making　**l.** weaving

Turn right at the first intersection.　Unit 10

▶ このユニットでは道案内に関する表現を学びます。

Warm-up

Trial　以下の表現を英語で考えてみましょう。

1. 「左側に郵便局が見えますよ」

---

2. 「最初の交差点を右折してください」

Useful Words　1〜8の語句の意味をa〜hから選びましょう。また、音声を聞いて発音も確認しましょう。

1. get to (　)　**2.** intersection (　)　**3.** just past (　)　**4.** keep *doing* (　)
5. left (　)　**6.** right (　)　**7.** traffic light (　)　**8.** until (　)

> **a.** …し続ける　**b.** …に着く　**c.** …まで　**d.** …を過ぎてすぐ
> **e.** 右　　　　**f.** 交差点　　**g.** 左　　　　**h.** 信号

1st Dialogue

Dictation 旅行者と観光ボランティアの会話を聞き、下線部に単語を記入しましょう。

Tourist: I'd like to go to the post office.
Volunteer: OK. Go ¹._____ and turn left at the second ²._____ _____. You'll see the post office on your ³._____.
Tourist: Go ¹._____ and turn left at the second ²._____ _____, and it's on the ³._____ side, correct?

Speaking ペアを組んで以下の会話を練習しましょう。Tourist は黒字部分を枠内の語句と入れ替えて伝え、Volunteer は黒字部分を自由に変えて目的地に案内しましょう。Tourist は地図内に目的地の名称を記入しましょう。さまざまなペアで練習を繰り返しましょう。

I'd like to go to the **post office**.

OK. Go **straight** and turn **left** at the **second** traffic light. It's on your **right**.

Tourist | Volunteer

post office
bank
pharmacy
convenience store
souvenir shop
tourist information center

HERE

2nd Dialogue

Dictation 旅行者と観光ボランティアの会話を聞き、下線部に単語を記入しましょう。

Tourist: Could you tell me how to ¹._____ _____ the karaoke place?

Volunteer: Sure. Turn right at the first ²._____. It's ³._____ _____ the computer store.

Tourist: OK. Thanks.

Speaking ペアを組んで以下の会話を練習しましょう。Touristは黒字部分を枠内の語句と入れ替えて伝え、Volunteerは黒字部分を自由に変えて目的地に案内しましょう。Touristは地図内に目的地の名称を記入しましょう。さまざまなペアで練習を繰り返しましょう。

Could you tell me how to get to the **karaoke place**?

Sure. Turn **right** at the **first** **intersection**. It's just past the **computer store**.

	hair salon	drugstore		cafe		burger restaurant	
	florist		bicycle shop	convenience store	ramen shop		
gas station		bank		computer store	karaoke place	post office	

HERE

karaoke place
supermarket
souvenir shop
manga cafe
bookstore
bakery

Listening

A 旅行者と観光ボランティアの会話を聞き、下線部に単語を記入して道案内を完成させましょう。 🎧70

To go to Hanshin Mall, first, go ¹._____ until you see Matsui ²._____. Then, turn ³._____ at the ⁴._____ traffic light just past Matsui ²._____. Keep walking, and you will see Hanshin Mall on your ⁵._____.

B 旅行者と観光ボランティアの会話を聞き、下線部に単語を記入して道案内を完成させましょう。 🎧71

To go to Kabuki Theater, first, turn ¹._____ at the first ²._____, then make a ³._____ at the next ²._____. Then, go straight for ⁴._____ or ⁵._____ blocks until you see the police box. Kabuki Theater is just ⁶._____ the police box, before the ⁷._____.

Useful Information 🎧72

[道案内時の目印となる公共施設や店舗]
- bakery「パン屋」 ● bookstore「本屋」 ● city hall「市役所、市庁舎」
- fire station「消防署」 ● florist「花屋」 ● gas station「ガソリンスタンド」
- hair salon「美容室」 ● hospital「病院」 ● mall「商店街、ショッピングセンター」
- *manga* cafe「マンガ喫茶」 ● park「公園」 ● pharmacy「薬局」 ● police box「交番」
- police station「警察署」 ● post office「郵便局」 ● souvenir shop「土産物店」

Unit 10

Turn right at the first intersection.

Roleplay

Student A スクリプト ▶ p.122

Tourist

あなたはTouristです。スクリプトの下線部1に目的地の名称を入れてVolunteerに伝えましょう。2、3にはVolunteerから聞いた情報を入れて行き方を確認し、以下の地図内に目的地の名称を記入しましょう。Tourist役を3回行いましょう。

	1
1st Time	Motoyoshi Theater
2nd Time	B's Manga Cafe
3rd Time	Ramen Toshi

Volunteer

今度はあなたがVolunteerです。スクリプトの下線部1はTouristの目的地、4は進み過ぎたことを示す建物名です。以下の地図を見ながら、2には目印となる建物名を、3、5にはrightかleftを入れて道案内しましょう。Volunteer役を3回行いましょう。

	1	4
1st Time	Hannan Park	Smile Hair Salon
2nd Time	Junpei's Souvenir Shop	Florist Hana
3rd Time	Funsound Karaoke	West High School

Roleplay

Student B スクリプト ▶ p.122

Volunteer

あなたはVolunteerです。スクリプトの下線1はTouristの目的地、4は進み過ぎたことを示す建物名です。以下の地図を見ながら、2には目印となる建物名を、3、5にはrightかleftを入れて道案内しましょう。Volunteer役を3回行いましょう。

	1	4
1st Time	Motoyoshi Theater	Matsui Bank
2nd Time	B's Manga Cafe	Smile Hair Salon
3rd Time	Ramen Toshi	Asahi Gas

Tourist

今度はあなたがTouristです。スクリプトの下線部1に目的地の名称を入れてVolunteerに伝えましょう。2、3にはVolunteerから聞いた情報を入れて行き方を確認し、以下の地図内に目的地の名称を記入しましょう。Tourist役を3回行いましょう。

	1
1st Time	Hannan Park
2nd Time	Junpei's Souvenir Shop
3rd Time	Funsound Karaoke

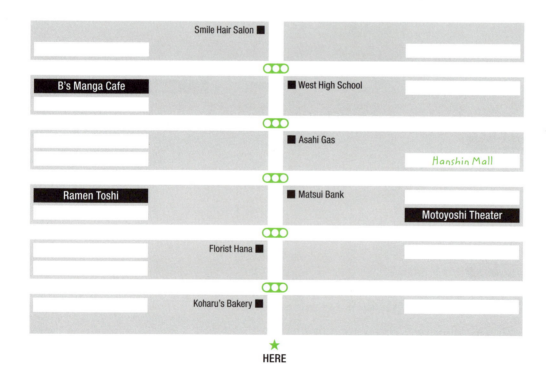

Reading

▼ 以下のパッセージを読み、質問に英文で答えましょう。

More than Just *Manga*

If you are visiting Japan because you like their *anime* or *manga*, a *manga* cafe is the place for you. You can choose your favorite *manga* from their huge collection, and then can enjoy reading it on a comfortable sofa with an all-you-can-drink service. Like regular cafes, they offer some food, from light snacks to full meals, as well as dessert. Also, you can access the Internet, check e-mail, play video games, or watch *anime* DVDs. Some cafes offer darts, billiards, and even karaoke. Many *manga* cafes have private booths so that you can relax. Some even have showers where you can refresh yourself. In fact, some local Japanese who miss the last train sometimes sleep there. In some travel guidebooks, a *manga* cafe is introduced as the cheapest accommodation. What is the rate? It is actually quite reasonable. An overnight stay of eight to ten hours costs as low as 1,500 yen. You should check them out!

NOTES ▶ all-you-can-drink service「飲み放題のサービス」 booth「ブース、仕切られた部屋」 accommodation「宿泊施設」

1. What do *manga* cafes offer that is like regular cafes?

2. What else can you do besides read *manga*? Give more than two examples.

3. What do some cafes offer? Give more than two examples.

4. How do some local Japanese people use a *manga* cafe?

5. How much does it cost to stay overnight?

Special Activity — Map Symbol

A 地図記号には日本独自のものもあります。1〜8の記号の意味をa〜hから選びましょう。

1 ( )　　2 ( )　　3 ( )　　4 ( )

5 ( )　　6 ( )　　7 ( )　　8 ( )

a. hospital
b. hot spring
c. museum
d. police box
e. post office
f. school
g. shrine
h. temple

B 以下の地図を見ながら1〜6の英文を完成させましょう。下線部には地図記号が表す建物などの名称または位置を示す語句が入ります。同じ名称は1度しか使えません。

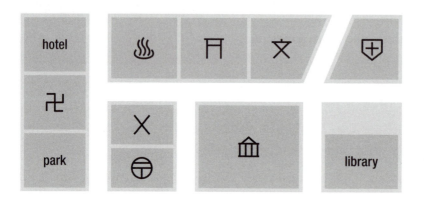

1　The hotel is _____ from the _____.
2　The _____ is _____ to the school.
3　The _____ is _____ the hotel and the park.
4　The library is in _____ of the _____.
5　The _____ is behind the _____.
6　The _____ is on the corner.

Take the subway to Hommachi.

Unit 11

▶ このユニットでは交通機関の利用案内や観光施設の情報提供に関する表現を学びます。

Warm-up

Trial 以下の表現を英語で考えてみましょう。

1. 「本町まで地下鉄に乗ってください」

_____

2. 「バスで20分ほどかかります」

_____

Useful Words 1〜8の語句の意味をa〜hから選びましょう。また、音声を聞いて発音も確認しましょう。 74

1. except (　)   2. get off (　)   3. hours (　)   4. miss (　)
5. sign (　)   6. stop (　)   7. ticket machine (　)   8. transfer (　)

> a. …以外   b. 見落とす   c. 表示、標識   d. 営業時間
> e. 降りる   f. 乗り換える   g. 券売機   h. 停車、停留所

1st Dialogue

Dictation 旅行者と観光ボランティアの会話を聞き、下線部に単語を記入しましょう。

Tourist: Excuse me. How do I get to the ¹._____?

Volunteer: OK. Take the Chuo ²._____ to Hommachi. It's five ³._____ from here.

Tourist: Thanks.

Volunteer: The ⁴._____ _____ are over there.

Speaking ペアを組んで以下の会話を練習しましょう。Volunteerは黒字部分を自由に変えて説明し、Touristはその内容を表に記入しましょう。さまざまなペアで練習を繰り返しましょう。

Tourist

Excuse me. How do I get to the **museum**?

Volunteer

OK. Take the **Chuo** Line to Hommachi. It's **five** stop(s) from here.

Ex.	Chuo	/	five
		/	
		/	
		/	
		/	
		/	
		/	
		/	

Take the subway to Hommachi. **11**

2nd Dialogue

Dictation 旅行者と観光ボランティアの会話を聞き、下線部に単語を記入しましょう。

Tourist: 1._____ _____ does it take to get to the aquarium?
Volunteer: Uh, it takes about 20 minutes by 2._____.
Tourist: Do you know their 3._____?
Volunteer: Let me check…, they are open from 9:00 a.m. to 7:00 p.m. 4._____ Mondays.

Speaking ペアを組んで以下の会話を練習しましょう。Touristは黒字部分を枠内の語句と入れ替えて質問し、Volunteerは自分で考えた所要時間を伝えてから目的地の名称を表に記入しましょう。さまざまなペアで練習を繰り返しましょう。

Tourist: How long does it take to get to the **aquarium**?

Volunteer: Uh, it takes about **20 minutes by bus**.

Ex. *aquarium*

aquarium
zoo
castle
temple
shrine
theater
tower

Listening

A 旅行者と観光ボランティアの会話を聞き、質問に英語で答えましょう。

1. Where does the tourist want to go?

2. What Line should the tourist transfer to?

3. How many stops is it from Hommachi to Morinomiya?

B 旅行者と観光ボランティアの会話を聞き、質問に英語で答えましょう。

1. How long does it take to get to the zoo?

2. How will the tourist probably get to the zoo?

3. What day is the zoo closed?

Useful Information

[移動手段に関する表現]
- You can go there by (bullet train / limited express / train / subway / monorail / ferry / bus / taxi).
「そこには (新幹線 / 特急 / 電車 / 地下鉄 / モノレール / フェリー / バス / タクシー) で行くことができます」
- It takes about 15 minutes on foot.
「歩いて15分くらいです」

[乗車券に関する表現]
- fare「運賃」　● ticket「(普通)乗車券、切符」　● express ticket「特急券」
- one-way ticket「片道切符」　● round-trip ticket「往復切符、周遊券」
- reserved seat「指定席」　● non-reserved seat「自由席」

Roleplay

Student A スクリプト ▶ p.124

Take the subway to Hommachi. Unit 11

Tourist

あなたはTouristで名古屋駅にいます。スクリプトの下線部1には目的地となる以下の名称を入れましょう。3は乗換駅、6は降車駅の名称です。2、5にはVolunteerから聞いた路線のアルファベット1文字を、4、7には停車駅の数を記入し、目的地までの行き方をVolunteerに確認しましょう。Tourist役を3回行いましょう。

	1	2	3	4	5	6	7
1st Time	Nagoya Castle		Sakae			Meijo Koen	
2nd Time	Osu Kannon		Fushimi			Osu Kannon	
3rd Time	Nagoya Dome		Hisaya-odori			Nagoya Dome-mae Yada	

Volunteer

今度はあなたがVolunteerで梅田駅にいます。スクリプトの下線部1に入る名称はTouristの目的地、3は乗換駅、6は降車駅の名称です。以下の路線図を見ながら、2、5には路線のアルファベット1文字を、4、7には停車駅の数を入れて目的地までの行き方をTouristに案内しましょう。Volunteer役を3回行いましょう。

	1	3	6
1st Time	Tsutenkaku Tower	Dobutsuen-mae	Ebisucho
2nd Time	Bunraku Theater	Namba	Nippombashi
3rd Time	Osaka Aquarium	Hommachi	Osakako

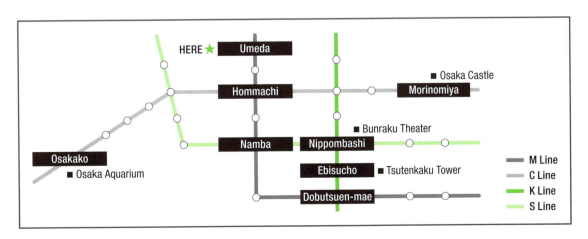

Roleplay

Student B スクリプト ▶ p.124

Volunteer あなたはVolunteerで名古屋駅にいます。スクリプトの下線部1に入る名称はTouristの目的地、3は乗換駅、6は降車駅の名称です。以下の路線図を見ながら、2、5には路線のアルファベット1文字を、4、7には停車駅の数を入れて目的地までの行き方をTouristに案内しましょう。Volunteer役を3回行いましょう。

	1	3	6
1st Time	Nagoya Castle	Sakae	Meijo Koen
2nd Time	Osu Kannon	Fushimi	Osu Kannon
3rd Time	Nagoya Dome	Hisaya-odori	Nagoya Dome-mae Yada

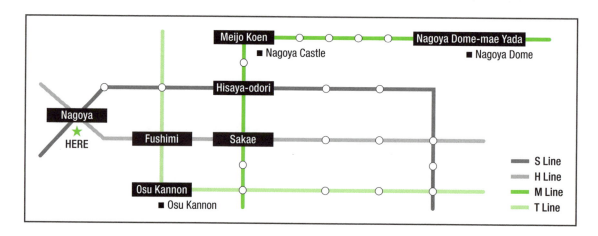

Tourist 今度はあなたがTouristで梅田駅にいます。スクリプトの下線部1には目的地となる以下の名称を入れましょう。3は乗換駅、6は降車駅の名称です。2、5にはVolunteerから聞いた路線のアルファベット1文字を、4、7には停車駅の数を記入し、目的地までの行き方をVolunteerに確認しましょう。Tourist役を3回行いましょう。

	1	2	3	4	5	6	7
1st Time	Tsutenkaku Tower		Dobutsuen-mae			Ebisucho	
2nd Time	Bunraku Theater		Namba			Nippombashi	
3rd Time	Osaka Aquarium		Hommachi			Osakako	

Reading

 以下のパッセージを読み、質問に英文で答えましょう。

Vending Machines Are Everywhere Selling almost Everything

Do you know how many vending machines there are in Japan? Japan has around 3.8 million machines across the whole country, which is about one for every 33 people. One of the reasons why there are so many is because Japan is quite a safe country, and no one worries about machines being vandalized, even in rural areas. These vending machines mostly sell beverages, but you can also buy some unique items from them, for example, eggs, rice, and light meals such as *takoyaki*, instant noodles, and rice balls. You can even buy underwear, *dashi* broth, and fresh fruit! What is more surprising, you can create and get personalized business cards from a vending machine if you forget yours on your business trip. While traveling throughout the country, you may run into very interesting vending machines. You never know what you can buy from them.

NOTES vandalize「故意に壊す」 rural「田舎の」 run into「…に出くわす」

1. How many vending machines are there in Japan?

2. What does no one worry about?

3. What do vending machines usually sell?

4. What are some unique items you can buy from vending machines? Give more than three examples.

5. If you forget your business cards, what can you do?

Special Activity: Transportation

A 選択肢の中から適語を選び、「DOCCAカード」の外国人旅行者向けの広告文を完成させましょう。文頭の単語は大文字で始めましょう。

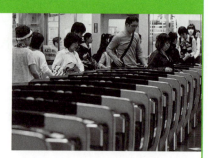

Get a DOCCA card—a 1._____ card not only to pay for 2._____ but also to be used as 3._____ money!

- 4._____ one at any train station for 2,000 yen!
- 5._____ it at a ticket machine. Very easy and fast!
- Don't forget to 6._____ the card when going home. You will 7._____ 500 yen back. Or keep the card for your 8._____ visit.

| buy | charge | electronic | fares | next | pre-paid | receive | return |

B a〜eの英文を並び替え、電車の乗り方の説明を完成させましょう。

1( ) → **2**( ) → **3**( ) → **4**( ) → **5**( )

a. Follow the sign to your platform.
b. Get on the train quickly. Hold a hanging strap if you are standing.
c. Go through the automatic gate. You need a ticket or a pre-paid card.
d. While waiting to board, wait in two lines.
e. When your train arrives, let passengers off first.

First, put money in the machine.

Unit 12

▶ このユニットでは券売機や電化製品の使用方法の説明に関する表現を学びます。

Warm-up

Trial 以下の表現を英語で考えてみましょう。

1. 「まず、機械にお金を入れてください」

_____

2. 「テレビをつけるには、このボタンを押してください」

_____

Useful Words 1〜8の語句の意味をa〜hから選びましょう。また、音声を聞いて発音も確認しましょう。

1. adjust (　)
2. air conditioner (　)
3. character (　)
4. destination (　)
5. dial (　)
6. press (　)
7. remote control (　)
8. temperature (　)

> a. エアコン　b. 文字　c. (電話を) かける　d. 調整する
> e. 目的地　f. リモコン　g. 押す　h. 温度

1st Dialogue

Dictation 旅行者とその場に居合わせた人の会話を聞き、下線部に単語を記入しましょう。

Tourist: Excuse me. Could you ¹._____ me with this?
Bystander: Sure. First, ²._____ money in the ³._____.
Tourist: Uh huh.
Bystander: Then, ⁴._____ the ⁵._____ you want to go to.

Speaking ペアを組んで以下の会話を練習しましょう。Bystanderは黒字部分を枠内の語句と入れ替えて説明し、Touristはその内容を表に記入しましょう。さまざまなペアで練習を繰り返しましょう。

Bystander

First, put money in the machine.

Then, select the **destination** you want to **go to**.

Tourist

Uh huh.

Ex.	destination	/	go to
		/	
		/	
		/	
		/	
		/	
		/	
		/	

destination / go to
movie / watch
show / watch
food / eat
menu item / have
ticket / buy
seat / take
time / travel

2nd Dialogue

Dictation ホテルのベル係と客の会話を聞き、下線部に単語を記入しましょう。客が尋ねている文字は「電源」です。

Bell Person: To turn on the TV, ^{1.}_____ this ^{2.}_____.
Guest: OK. What do these ^{3.}_____ mean?
Bell Person: They mean ^{4.}_____.
Guest: Thanks.

Speaking ペアを組んで以下の会話を練習しましょう。Bell Personは黒字部分を枠内の語句と入れ替えて伝え、Guestはその内容を表に記入しましょう。さまざまなペアで練習を繰り返しましょう。

To **turn on the TV**, press this button.

Bell Person

OK, thanks.

Guest

Ex. *turn on the TV*

turn on the TV
turn on the electricity
flush the toilet
use the air conditioner
take a shower
use hot water
display English
dial an outside line

Listening

A 旅行者とその場に居合わせた人の会話を聞きましょう。設問1、2は質問に英語で答え、3は下線部に単語を記入して答えを完成させましょう。 🎧84

1. Where is this conversation most likely taking place?
   _____

2. How many tickets did the tourist buy?
   _____

3. What did the tourist take last?

   The tickets and _____.

B ホテルのベル係と客の会話を聞き、質問に英語で答えましょう。 🎧85

1. How can the guest adjust the temperature?
   _____

2. What characters are most likely being discussed? Write the *kanji* characters.
   _____

3. What number should the guest dial if she needs anything?
   _____

Useful Information 🎧86

[一般的な電化製品]
- coffee maker「コーヒーメーカー」 ● drier「乾燥機」 ● fan「換気扇、扇風機」
- heater「ヒーター」 ● hot water dispenser「電気ポット」 ● humidifier「加湿器」
- microwave「電子レンジ」 ● refrigerator「冷蔵庫」 ● rice cooker「炊飯器」
- vacuum cleaner「掃除機」 ● washing machine「洗濯機」

Roleplay

Student A スクリプト ▶ p.124

First, put money in the machine.

Unit 12

Bell Person あなたはBell Personです。スクリプトの下線部1～4に以下の情報を入れてGuestに伝えましょう。Bell Person役を3回行いましょう。

	1	2	3	4
1st Time	1105	watch DVDs	POWER	5
2nd Time	204	display English	VOLUME	1
3rd Time	903	turn off the TV	MENU	3

Guest 今度はあなたがGuestです。以下の1、4にBell Personから聞いた部屋番号と内線番号を記入し、2、3はBell Personから聞いた情報にチェックをつけましょう。Guest役を3回行いましょう。

	1	2	3	4
1st Time		☐ play video games ☐ turn up the volume ☐ display English	☐ CANCEL ☐ CHANNEL ☐ STOP	
2nd Time		☐ turn off the TV ☐ turn up the volume ☐ watch the hotel guide	☐ MENU ☐ SWITCH ☐ MUTE	
3rd Time		☐ play video games ☐ turn up the volume ☐ watch DVDs	☐ PLAY ☐ RECORD ☐ RETURN	

Roleplay

Student B スクリプト ▶ p.124

Guest　あなたはGuestです。以下の1、4にBell Personから聞いた部屋番号と内線番号を記入し、2、3はBell Personから聞いた情報にチェックをつけましょう。Guest役を3回行いましょう。

	1	2	3	4
1st Time		☐ turn up the volume ☐ watch DVDs ☐ watch the hotel guide	☐ PAUSE ☐ RECORD ☐ POWER	
2nd Time		☐ display English ☐ play video games ☐ turn off the TV	☐ CHANNEL ☐ VOLUME ☐ RETURN	
3rd Time		☐ watch the hotel guide ☐ turn up the volume ☐ turn off the TV	☐ MENU ☐ RECORD ☐ MUTE	

Bell Person　今度はあなたがBell Personです。スクリプトの下線部1〜4に以下の情報を入れてGuestに伝えましょう。Bell Person役を3回行いましょう。

	1	2	3	4
1st Time	701	turn up the volume	CHANNEL	8
2nd Time	1508	watch the hotel guide	MUTE	0
3rd Time	512	play video games	RETURN	7

Reading

▼ 以下のパッセージを読み、質問に英文で答えましょう。

Unique Souvenirs for Just 100 Yen

You have enjoyed your stay in Japan, now it is time to go home. In other words, it is time to find souvenirs. Try a 100 yen shop! 100 yen shops are like dollar stores in the U.S. Cosmetics, snacks, kitchenware, stationery, and toys are just a few of the many different kinds of products they offer. Now, let's take a look at some typical souvenirs you can buy there: chopsticks, washcloths, tea cups, and *maneki-neko* dolls. Also, you can find some unique gifts such as *ninja* stickers, iPhone covers with traditional Japanese designs, and *bento* boxes. If you are interested in cooking, you can even get a sushi mold. With this, you can make beautiful sushi quite easily. Each item is only 100 yen, so you might end up spending much more than you had planned.

NOTES ▶ kitchenware「台所用品」 stationery「文房具」 mold「型」 end up -ing「結局…となる」

1. What is sold in 100 yen shops? Give a few examples.

2. What are some typical souvenirs? Give a few examples.

3. What are some unique souvenirs?

4. What is suggested for someone who likes cooking?

5. Why might a tourist spend more than they had planned?

Special Activity: Controller

A 下線部に適切な語または数字を入れて、エアコンの操作パネルの使い方の説明文を完成させましょう。

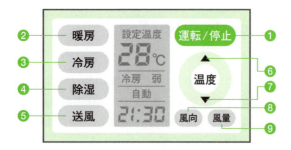

1. To turn on the air conditioner, press the button _____.
2. To switch to _____, press the button ❸.
3. To switch to DRY, press the button _____.
4. To change the direction of the wind, press the button _____.
5. To turn _____ the temperature, press the button ❼.
6. To turn _____ the air conditioner, press the button ❶.

B 下線部に適切な数字を入れて、電気ポットの操作ボタンの使い方の説明文を完成させましょう。

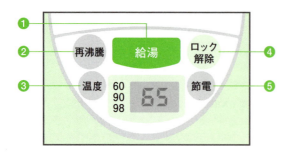

1. To boil again, press the button _____.
2. To unlock, press the button _____.
3. To save power, press the button _____.
4. To dispense hot water, press the button _____.

Review 2　　　　　　　　　　　　　　　　　　　　Units 7–12

Key Vocabulary

A　1～12の語句の意味をa～lから選びましょう。

1. adjust　　　　（　）　　7. miss　　　　　（　）
2. budget　　　　（　）　　8. recommend　（　）
3. destination　（　）　　9. reserve　　　（　）
4. insert　　　　（　）　　10. specialty　　（　）
5. intersection（　）　　11. traffic light（　）
6. look for　　　（　）　　12. transfer　　　（　）

> a. …を探す　　b. 差し込む　　c. 勧める　　d. 見落とす
> e. 交差点　　　f. 乗り換える　g. 信号　　　h. 調整する
> i. 名産品　　　j. 目的地　　　k. 予算　　　l. 予約する

B　英語は日本語に、日本語は英語にしましょう。

1. deep-fried pork　　　　→ _____
2. grilled chicken skewer → _____
3. rice cooker　　　　　　→ _____
4. rice cracker　　　　　　→ _____
5. 抹茶クッキー　　　　　　→ _____ _____
6. 神社　　　　　　　　　　→ _____
7. 城　　　　　　　　　　　→ _____
8. 温泉　　　　　　　　　　→ _____

Key Expressions

A [ ]内の語句を並べ替え、以下の表現を英語にしましょう。ただし不足している1語は自分で追加し、文頭の単語は大文字で始めましょう。

1. 「こちらの用紙に記入していただけますか」
   [could / form / out / this / you / ?]

2. 「恐縮ですが、コピー機はございません」
   [a / copy / don't / have / I'm / machine / we / .]

3. 「ここから徒歩で5分のところに美しいお寺がありますよ」
   [a five-minute / beautiful / here / is / just / from / there / walk / a / .]

4. 「左側に郵便局が見えますよ」
   [office / post / you'll / your / on / see / the / .]

5. 「バスで20分ほどかかります」
   [20 / about / by / it / minutes / bus / .]

6. 「テレビをつけるには、このボタンを押してください」
   [button / on / the / this / to / turn / TV / , / .]

B 1～6の英文を聞き、それぞれの応答として最も適切なものをa～hから選びましょう。 🎧88

1. ( )　2. ( )　3. ( )　4. ( )　5. ( )　6. ( )

- a. About 1,500 yen per person.
- b. Correct.
- c. I highly recommend Sakura Restaurant.
- d. It's available in this area.
- e. Put money in the machine.
- f. Take the M Line to Hommachi.
- g. They mean CANCEL.
- h. Yes. I'm Penny Brown.

Listening

A 旅行者と観光ボランティアの会話を聞き、質問に英語で答えましょう。 🎧89

1. Where does the tourist want to go?

2. How long does it take to get there?

3. What kind of restaurant did the volunteer recommend?

B ホテルのベル係と客の会話を聞き、質問に英語で答えましょう。 🎧90

1. What characters are most likely being discussed? Write the *kanji* characters.

2. Where is Wi-Fi available?

3. Where is an ATM?

Reading

▼ 次の英文を読み、Units 7〜12のパッセージの内容と一致する場合はT、一致しない場合はFを○で囲みましょう。

1. In many countries, you remove all your clothes when you bathe in a public bath. [T / F]
2. You can bathe in an open-air bath looking at the beautiful sky in Japan. [T / F]
3. None of the toilet lids in Japan open automatically. [T / F]
4. You may hear a fake flushing sound when you use a public toilet in Japan. [T / F]
5. Recently, only monks are allowed to stay in temple lodgings, or *shukubo*. [T / F]
6. Hand-copying a Buddhist sutra is called *shakyo*. [T / F]
7. At a *manga* cafe, you can enjoy not just *manga*, but also food. [T / F]
8. A *manga* cafe is not as reasonable as you think. [T / F]
9. You can buy many different things from vending machines in Japan. [T / F]
10. In rural areas, some people vandalize vending machines in Japan. [T / F]
11. A 100 yen shop is a good place to get souvenirs. [T / F]
12. At a 100 yen shop, you never spend much money because each item is only 100 yen. [T / F]

Model Conversation — Unit 1

Clerk: Are you ready to order?
Customer: Yes. I'll have a ¹fish burger set.
Clerk: OK. All the burgers come with a small drink, and French fries or a salad. Which would you like?
Customer: Then, I'll have a salad.
Clerk: OK. What type of dressing would you like? We have ²Japanese, Italian, and sesame.
Customer: I'll try ³Japanese.
Clerk: OK. What drink would you like?
Customer: I'll have ⁴orange juice.

Model Conversation — Unit 2

Server: Hello. Do you have a reservation?
Guest: No. Do you have any openings?
Server: How many are in your party?
Guest: ¹Four.
Server: Would you like smoking or non-smoking? We only have some ²smoking seats available now.
Guest: We'd like ³non-smoking, please.
Server: OK, then, could you please wait for about ⁴15 minutes?
Guest: Sure.
Server: Please write your name on this waiting list.

Roleplay Script — Unit 1

Clerk: Are you ready to order?
Customer: Yes. I'll have a [1]_____ set.
Clerk: OK. All the burgers come with a small drink, and French fries or a salad. Which would you like?
Customer: Then, I'll have a salad.
Clerk: OK. What type of dressing would you like? We have [2]_____.
Customer: I'll try [3]_____.
Clerk: OK. What drink would you like?
Customer: I'll have [4]_____.

Roleplay Script — Unit 2

Server: Hello. Do you have a reservation?
Guest: No. Do you have any openings?
Server: How many are in your party?
Guest: [1]_____.
Server: Would you like smoking or non-smoking? We only have some [2]_____ seats available now.
Guest: We'd like [3]_____, please.
Server: OK, then, could you please wait for about [4]_____ minutes?
Guest: Sure.
Server: Please write your name on this waiting list.

Model Conversation — Unit 3

Server: This is the ¹Zarusoba Special.
Guest: Thanks. Oh, what is this for?
Server: It's the sauce for ²buckwheat noodles. Please dip them in this sauce.
Guest: I see. Now, what are these?
Server: They are ³wasabi, green onions, and dried seaweed. You can mix them into the sauce if you'd like.
Guest: All right. I'll try it.
Server: Enjoy your meal.

Model Conversation — Unit 4

Clerk: Is that all for today?
Customer: Uh, I'll also take this ¹donut.
Clerk: OK. How many would you like?
Customer: ²Three.
Clerk: Sure. Would you like me to heat up this boxed lunch?
Customer: That will be great.
Clerk: Could you wait for a moment?
Customer: No problem. Also, I'd like to have ³two large cups for hot coffee.
Clerk: Here you go. Anything else?
Customer: No.
Clerk: OK. Here is your boxed lunch. It's hot, so please be careful.

Roleplay Script — Unit 3

Server: This is the ¹_____ Special.
Guest: Thanks. Oh, what is this for?
Server: It's the sauce for ²_____. Please dip them in this sauce.
Guest: I see. Now, what are these?
Server: They are ³_____. You can mix them into the sauce if you'd like.
Guest: All right. I'll try it.
Server: Enjoy your meal.

Roleplay Script — Unit 4

Clerk: Is that all for today?
Customer: Uh, I'll also take this ¹_____.
Clerk: OK. How many would you like?
Customer: ²_____.
Clerk: Sure. Would you like me to heat up this boxed lunch?
Customer: That will be great.
Clerk: Could you wait for a moment?
Customer: No problem. Also, I'd like to have ³_____.
Clerk: Here you go. Anything else?
Customer: No.
Clerk: OK. Here is your boxed lunch. It's hot, so please be careful.

Model Conversation — Unit 5

Cashier: Did you find everything OK today?
Customer: Yes.
Cashier: OK. ¹2,280 yen, ²1,530 yen, and ³3,980 yen...plus tax...your total comes to ⁴8,413 yen.
Customer: Here.
Cashier: I'll take ⁴8,413 yen out of ⁵10,000 yen. ⁶1,587 yen is your change.
Customer: Is it possible to return goods?
Cashier: Yes, but you need the receipt. Please return the item with the receipt within ⁷a week.
Customer: OK, thanks.
Cashier: Have a nice day.

Model Conversation — Unit 6

Customer: Hi. I bought this yesterday.
Clerk: Do you have the receipt?
Customer: Here. This is ¹the wrong size.
Clerk: We're terribly sorry. We can exchange it. Let me check if we have another one. Just a moment, please.
Customer: OK.
....
Clerk: I'm very sorry. This item is out of stock now. It's coming back in stock ²next Monday.
Customer: Then, could I get a refund?
Clerk: Certainly. Again, I apologize for the inconvenience.

Roleplay Script — Unit 5

Cashier: Did you find everything OK today?
Customer: Yes.
Cashier: OK. ¹_____ yen, ²_____ yen, and ³_____ yen…plus tax…your total comes to ⁴_____ yen.
Customer: Here.
Cashier: I'll take ⁴_____ yen out of ⁵_____ yen. ⁶_____ yen is your change.
Customer: Is it possible to return goods?
Cashier: Yes, but you need the receipt. Please return the item with the receipt within ⁷_____.
Customer: OK, thanks.
Cashier: Have a nice day.

Roleplay Script — Unit 6

Customer: Hi. I bought this yesterday.
Clerk: Do you have the receipt?
Customer: Here. This is ¹_____.
Clerk: We're terribly sorry. We can exchange it. Let me check if we have another one. Just a moment, please.
Customer: OK.

....

Clerk: I'm very sorry. This item is out of stock now. It's coming back in stock ²_____.
Customer: Then, could I get a refund?
Clerk: Certainly. Again, I apologize for the inconvenience.

Model Conversation — Unit 7

Desk Clerk: Hello, may I help you?
Guest: Hi. I'd like to check in.
Desk Clerk: Certainly. Do you have a reservation?
Guest: Yes. I'm ¹Tina Kane.
Desk Clerk: ²Ms. Kane. Let me see…, your reservation is for a ³single room for ⁴two nights, right?
Guest: That's right. Is that a ⁵non-smoking room?
Desk Clerk: Uh…, I'm afraid it isn't. Would you prefer a ⁵non-smoking room?
Guest: Yes, please.
Desk Clerk: Just one moment, please.

Model Conversation — Unit 8

Desk Clerk: Hello, can I help you?
Guest: Hi. Do you have ¹some medicine for a headache?
Desk Clerk: I'm afraid we don't, but there is ²a drugstore next to the station.
Guest: OK, thanks.
Desk Clerk: Is there anything else I could help you with?
Guest: Well, I'm looking for some typical Japanese souvenirs. Do you have any ideas?
Desk Clerk: Sure. A specialty of this area is ³shrimp crackers. They are very popular among foreign tourists.
Guest: Thanks.

Roleplay Script — Unit 7

Desk Clerk: Hello, may I help you?
Guest: Hi. I'd like to check in.
Desk Clerk: Certainly. Do you have a reservation?
Guest: Yes. I'm [1]_____.
Desk Clerk: [2]_____. Let me see…, your reservation is for a [3]_____ room for [4]_____, right?
Guest: That's right. Is that a [5]_____?
Desk Clerk: Uh…, I'm afraid it isn't. Would you prefer a [5]_____?
Guest: Yes, please.
Desk Clerk: Just one moment, please.

Roleplay Script — Unit 8

Desk Clerk: Hello, can I help you?
Guest: Hi. Do you have [1]_____?
Desk Clerk: I'm afraid we don't, but there is [2]_____.
Guest: OK, thanks.
Desk Clerk: Is there anything else I could help you with?
Guest: Well, I'm looking for some typical Japanese souvenirs. Do you have any ideas?
Desk Clerk: Sure. A specialty of this area is [3]_____. They are very popular among foreign tourists.
Guest: Thanks.

Model Conversation — Unit 9

Tourist: Hi. Is there a nice restaurant around here?
Volunteer: OK. What kind of food would you like? There are Japanese, Chinese, Italian, French, and Indian.
Tourist: We'd like to have Japanese.
Volunteer: Sure. What's your budget?
Tourist: About [1]1,500 yen per person.
Volunteer: I see. Do you have any allergies?
Tourist: No.
Volunteer: Then, I highly recommend Akatsuki. They are a very [2]reasonable sushi restaurant.
Tourist: Actually, we had some sushi for lunch.
Volunteer: Well then, how about the [3]*soba* restaurant, [4]Haru? They serve the best [5]buckwheat noodles in this area.

Model Conversation — Unit 10

Tourist: I'd like to go to [1]Hanshin Mall.
Volunteer: OK. Well, go straight until you get to [2]Matsui Bank. Then, turn [3]right at the first traffic light.
Tourist: Turn [3]right at the first traffic light just past [2]Matsui Bank?
Volunteer: Right. If you get to [4]Asahi Gas, you've gone too far.
Tourist: OK, then?
Volunteer: After turning [3]right, just keep walking until you see [1]Hanshin Mall on your [5]left.

Roleplay Script — Unit 9

Tourist: Hi. Is there a nice restaurant around here?
Volunteer: OK. What kind of food would you like? There are Japanese, Chinese, Italian, French, and Indian.
Tourist: We'd like to have Japanese.
Volunteer: Sure. What's your budget?
Tourist: About [1]_____ yen per person.
Volunteer: I see. Do you have any allergies?
Tourist: No.
Volunteer: Then, I highly recommend Akatsuki. They are a very [2]_____ sushi restaurant.
Tourist: Actually, we had some sushi for lunch.
Volunteer: Well then, how about the [3]_____ restaurant, [4]_____? They serve the best [5]_____ in this area.

Roleplay Script — Unit 10

Tourist: I'd like to go to [1]_____.
Volunteer: OK. Well, go straight until you get to [2]_____. Then, turn [3]_____ at the first traffic light.
Tourist: Turn [3]_____ at the first traffic light just past [2]_____?
Volunteer: Right. If you get to [4]_____, you've gone too far.
Tourist: OK, then?
Volunteer: After turning [3]_____, just keep walking until you see [1]_____ on your [5]_____.

Model Conversation — Unit 11

Tourist: How do I get to ¹Osaka Castle?
Volunteer: OK. Take the ²M Line to ³Hommachi. It's ⁴two stops from here.
Tourist: Take the ²M Line and get off at ³Hommachi?
Volunteer: Right, and then transfer to the ⁵C Line to ⁶Morinomiya. It's ⁷three stops from ³Hommachi.
Tourist: At ³Hommachi, take the ⁵C Line to ⁶Morinomiya, right?
Volunteer: Correct.
Tourist: How do I get to ¹Osaka Castle from there?
Volunteer: You'll see a big sign at the station. You can't miss it.

Model Conversation — Unit 12

Bell Person: This is your room, ¹502. To turn on all the electricity, insert your key card here.
Guest: OK. How do I use the air conditioner?
Bell Person: To use the air conditioner, press this button. You can adjust the temperature with the remote control.
Guest: OK, thanks.
Bell Person: Now, the TV is over here. To ²turn on the TV, press this button.
Guest: What do these characters mean?
Bell Person: They mean ³ON and OFF.
Guest: All right.
Bell Person: If you need anything, just dial ⁴9 for assistance. Have a nice evening.

Roleplay Script — Unit 11

Tourist: How do I get to ¹_____?

Volunteer: OK. Take the ²_____ Line to ³_____. It's ⁴_____ stop(s) from here.

Tourist: Take the ²_____ Line and get off at ³_____?

Volunteer: Right, and then transfer to the ⁵_____ Line to ⁶_____. It's ⁷_____ stop(s) from ³_____.

Tourist: At ³_____, take the ⁵_____ Line to ⁶_____, right?

Volunteer: Correct.

Tourist: How do I get to ¹_____ from there?

Volunteer: You'll see a big sign at the station. You can't miss it.

Roleplay Script — Unit 12

Bell Person: This is your room, ¹_____. To turn on all the electricity, insert your key card here.

Guest: OK. How do I use the air conditioner?

Bell Person: To use the air conditioner, press this button. You can adjust the temperature with the remote control.

Guest: OK, thanks.

Bell Person: Now, the TV is over here. To ²_____, press this button.

Guest: What do these characters mean?

Bell Person: They mean ³_____.

Guest: All right.

Bell Person: If you need anything, just dial ⁴_____ for assistance. Have a nice evening.

Checklist

■以下の重要表現を英語で伝えられるか確認しましょう。

			初回	最終回
Unit 1		ファストフード店での注文対応		
	1	「ご注文はお決まりでしょうか」	☐	☐
	2	「こちらでお召し上がりでしょうか、お持ち帰りでしょうか」	☐	☐
Unit 2		レストランでの来客対応		
	3	「何名様でしょうか」	☐	☐
	4	「まず始めにお飲み物はいかがでしょうか」	☐	☐
Unit 3		レストランでの接客サービス		
	5	「こちらは魚貝類と野菜用のつゆでございます」	☐	☐
	6	「すぐにお持ちいたします」	☐	☐
Unit 4		コンビニやスーパーでの接客サービス		
	7	「お箸はいくつご入用ですか」	☐	☐
	8	「こちらを温めましょうか」	☐	☐
Unit 5		買い物や飲食の会計		
	9	「お支払いは3,240円になります」	☐	☐
	10	「現金かカード、どちらでのお支払いですか」	☐	☐
Unit 6		商品やサービスへの苦情対応		
	11	「ご迷惑をおかけして申し訳ございません」	☐	☐
	12	「他のものがあるか確認いたします」	☐	☐
Unit 7		ホテルや旅館での宿泊客受付		
	13	「ご予約はいただいておりますか」	☐	☐
	14	「こちらの用紙に記入していただけますか」	☐	☐
Unit 8		商業施設でのサービス提供や近隣情報の案内		
	15	「Wi-Fiはこちらのエリアでご利用可能です」	☐	☐
	16	「恐縮ですが、コピー機はございません」	☐	☐
Unit 9		旅行者への観光案内		
	17	「桜レストランが大変お勧めです」	☐	☐
	18	「ここから徒歩で5分のところに美しいお寺がありますよ」	☐	☐
Unit 10		道案内		
	19	「左側に郵便局が見えますよ」	☐	☐
	20	「最初の交差点を右折してください」	☐	☐
Unit 11		交通機関の利用案内や観光施設の情報提供		
	21	「本町まで地下鉄に乗ってください」	☐	☐
	22	「バスで20分ほどかかります」	☐	☐
Unit 12		券売機や電化製品の使用方法の説明		
	23	「まず、機械にお金を入れてください」	☐	☐
	24	「テレビをつけるには、このボタンを押してください」	☐	☐

■重要表現の英語を確認しましょう。

Unit 1	1	Are you ready to order?
	2	For here, or to go?
Unit 2	3	How many are in your party?
	4	Would you like some drinks to start with?
Unit 3	5	This is the sauce for seafood and vegetables.
	6	I'll be right back.
Unit 4	7	How many chopsticks do you need?
	8	Would you like me to heat this up?
Unit 5	9	Your total comes to 3,240 yen.
	10	Cash or credit card?
Unit 6	11	I'm truly sorry for the trouble.
	12	Let me check if we have another one.
Unit 7	13	Do you have a reservation?
	14	Could you fill out this form?
Unit 8	15	Wi-Fi is available in this area.
	16	I'm afraid we don't have a copy machine.
Unit 9	17	I highly recommend Sakura Restaurant.
	18	There is a beautiful temple just a five-minute walk from here.
Unit 10	19	You'll see the post office on your left.
	20	Turn right at the first intersection.
Unit 11	21	Take the subway to Hommachi.
	22	It takes about 20 minutes by bus.
Unit 12	23	First, put money in the machine.
	24	To turn on the TV, press this button.

教師用音声CD有り（非売品）

You're Welcome!
──Communication with Tourists Made Easy
すぐに使える！ ニッポン案内

2016年3月1日　初版発行
2023年3月30日　第 9 刷

著　者　　工藤多恵
発行者　　松村達生
発行所　　センゲージ ラーニング株式会社
　　　　　〒102-0073　東京都千代田区九段北1-11-11　第2フナトビル5階
　　　　　電話 03-3511-4392　FAX 03-3511-4391
　　　　　e-mail: eltjapan@cengage.com
　　　　　copyright©2016 センゲージ ラーニング株式会社

装　丁　　　　足立友幸(parastyle)
編集協力　　　飯尾緑子(parastyle)
イラスト　　　イチカワエリ
印刷・製本　　株式会社ムレコミュニケーションズ

ISBN 978-4-86312-279-6

もし落丁、乱丁、その他不良品がありましたら、お取り替えいたします。本書の全部または一部を無断で複写(コピー)することは、著作権法上での例外を除き、禁じられていますのでご注意ください。